Boston and Return

Gladys Brooks in 1920, drawing by John Singer Sargent

Boston and Return

GLADYS BROOKS

NEW YORK

ATHENEUM

1962

DEDICATED TO MY HUSBAND

VAN WYCK BROOKS

Contents

Boston and Return

I

VOLUNTARY

THERE is a poignant pleasure that comes in the writing of one's past, a pleasure which can be put to use provided the writer is able to see himself as he sees the leaves in autumn dropping one by one, year after year. The dying leaves speak of coming finality, but the persistence of their shape, intact until buried beneath winter snows, brings a reminder of springtime when first they opened to the sun, brings the promise of another springtime on ahead bright with new urgencies.

Thus does a life fluctuate between the past and the future, moving with a rhythm as regular as the denial and promise of earth, as repetitive as the drifting of the waves upon the shore, forward and back, forward and back. In the end it is difficult to choose between what leans backward and what lies ahead. Looking upon the sinuous line of one's being, which mingles events in their sequences and casts away dates that hamper the flow, one sets down the thing remembered and allows it so to stand, hoping that the beat of one's heart may, throughout, remain constant and true.

In the days that led to my marriage, as a girl, I questioned my mother about long-lasting stability, about the powers of endurance and loyalty.

"What is there to depend on?" I asked. "What of promises made to others, what of the continuity of love and hope? How can I be sure of these things?"

"You can be sure only of yourself, your own courage, your own strength, your own goodness," she had answered.

With these words of hers, in a book called *Gramercy Park,* I brought to a close an account of my New York girlhood. I was born in a wistaria-covered brick house on Irving Place, a block away from Gramercy Park. There, with my sister and brother, I spent the winters of my youth, attending the Brearley School and studying the violin under various masters. Our doctor father, a nose and throat specialist, had his office as a part of our house with the entrance around the corner on Nineteenth Street. Here, we children were once in a while permitted to penetrate and we delighted in the air of glamour spread about the rooms where the actors and singers of the day, impressive men and scent-appareled ladies, waited to have their vocal cords restored to order. When spring came, bringing the end of school, we left my father and his busy life and moved with my mother to East Hampton on Long Island to spend our summers in a house on a hill overlooking the sea. Several summers were spent in France and we children early learned to speak the French tongue, a fact that caused our parents much satisfaction. This had a bearing on our future, establishing in our hearts a long-lived love of France, and, for my brother, it became an element that held him a willing adjunct of the French army, first in the American Ambulance Service, later in the two World Wars. Now and then, usually during the school year, I went to visit my grandmother at Great Barrington in the Berkshires. These visits were to me like a journey into heaven because of the cherishing care bestowed upon me, the lull in strenuous labor, the freshness of air as I walked the upward path toward a mountaintop. It was here at my grandmother's that I was inspired to write my most serious compositions, handing them presently to Miss Dunn, teacher of English at the Brearley.

After I had become a young lady, enamored of the joyous round of dances, beaux, bouquets, and had had my own "coming out" dance in a candlelit studio in the East Forties, I began, with a companion, to make a serious study of the trees and shrubs of our land in order to become a professional landscape gardener. We studied at the Arnold Arboretum on the outskirts of Boston and we not only visited local gardens but we saw also many of the splendid gardens of England and France on a trip arranged for us by an aunt of my friend, a lady of widespread European acquaintance.

This trip may have influenced me more than I knew, for it threw me momentarily into a world of social importance, of affluence and power taken for granted, a world that flashed its brilliance in compelling fashion even while it repelled and alarmed me by the austerity of its rules and customs. On my return, almost at once, I met the man who was soon after to become my husband, a man of old New England stock, so good-looking, so assured in his position, so superior in bearing and character, that it seemed as though a benign and protecting fate had led me to him.

We were married when I was in my early twenties and I was taken to live in Boston. Here, the patterns of existence as I had learned them in childhood became negligible almost overnight. From informality and the values of an artist's world, I went at once into the ordered custom of the Boston patriarch, and, with an instinctive wish to be greeted with warmth, to be considered worthy of my husband, I strove with all my might to conform. Often I was bewildered but presently I emerged from confusion, and, with my violin to sustain me, and the help of new-found friends, I succeeded in finding my place a little outside the tightly knit society about me. Thus was the door temporarily shut on the unplanned, impulsive and more hazardous ways of being which had always been mine.

During the fifteen years that followed, crowded years, I bore and brought up my four children, ran a complex household and stood at my husband's side, enjoying my position there, absorbing the measure of my blessings as though they had been destined to endure forever. Indeed, an allegorical drawing made of me in the early years, a drawing in the shape of a nymph from whose hands spilled an overflowing horn of plenty, seemed a most fitting portrait.

The longing for things past, those inherent in childhood, I had nevertheless not managed to subdue. I was often unsure, moving inwardly in two directions, a compass veering from north to south, at first slowly, more abruptly as the years went by. To be thus torn was predestined for me. As a child I had fluctuated between the equal but disparate desires of my parents, desires as different in substance and texture as wool from silk, as copper from mahogany. Had there not always been a tug of war between my father's kindhearted but determined battle for worldly success and my mother's high-minded idealism that took account not only of morals but of the arts as well? Had I not, as I grew, despaired of telling right from wrong, longed to be guided in a single direction and thus find peace?

The battle of ideals had continued between the two, an undercurrent disturbingly apparent to me, when the young man from Boston had asked permission for my hand. My father had been gratified at the substantial prospect that beckoned for his eldest daughter, my mother less so. As we talked, she and I, of the proposal and my acceptance, even though she tried to give me her honest blessing, her eyebrows had been drawn to a sharp point in her forehead, the familiar sign denoting skepticism or downright disapproval.

"Do you think you'll have much in common as time goes on, you two? What will you be able to share?" she had asked.

"Oh, plenty of things," I had answered briskly, airily, stepping on top of the waves. "And all doors will be open to us wherever we go, here and in Europe."

"You may find, as I have, that only a very few doors are really worth entering, Gladys. But this each of us must discover for himself."

An outsider listening to our conversation might have found my mother's words unsympathetic, even harsh. But I knew they sprang from deep love and an ardent wish that I hitch my wagon to nothing less than Emerson's star.

And so, after the years—and the building of an apparently solid and indestructible edifice which contained my husband and the children dear to me—when my guiding star, happily or no, pointed in a far direction—a direction contrary to that in which I walked, whether forward or back—I did not resist. I followed the sign, accepting destiny as it led me through the long nightmare of solitude, of separation from those I loved, from devotion and safety and care and a conscience untroubled. I followed while, deep in my heart, a small voice whispered of life ahead, whispered of courage and compassion and the underlying unity for which man must ever strive.

I have come nearer to these things at last and can attempt to set down the story of experience seized almost at random, as the organist in his voluntary seizes upon contrapuntal sequences. The story moves from events that begin with childhood, thus attempting to clarify for the reader the pattern of early influences, and ends with the close of my first marriage. In the chapters which follow, the episodes are presented perhaps not as another might have perceived them. Memory is answerable to each of us in his own way and is ever in need of persuasion.

2

MARRONNIERS FLEURIS

WHEN we were young in Paris, my sister, my brother and I, we were taken more than once to the Musée de Cluny, a damp, dark place filled with the odor of medieval torture where hung the gibbet, the rack, the iron spikes, the branding iron and the chastity belt, a circular iron girdle the purpose of which our governess did not explain. Leaving the museum, emerging at last from the Middle Ages and into the bright May sunshine of our own world, we ate ices in a patisserie and walked home through the Luxembourg Garden where children played in sand piles and gardeners were forever busy with the ordering of flower beds, where sweet-smelling orange trees grew in tubs against the walls. Now and then, when the weather was rainy, our *Mademoiselle* hailed a fiacre and we sat below a red-faced coachman whose mustache was wet with beer, or another of cadaverous mien whose tall hat accentuated the height of his melancholy brow. I pitied the horses, half starved, with ribs showing as sharply as the ribs of the horses I was

later to see in the Spanish arena patiently waiting to be
gored, when my mother took me to the royal bullfight
at Madrid given in honor of the King and Queen of
Spain, she a recent English bride. I wondered then
whether the fair-haired young woman, unaccustomed to
southern frenzy, untutored in the savage arts, had suffered as had I at this first glimpse of the bloody sport. It
seemed a sad opening to the long days she was to spend
in her adopted land.

On fair days in Paris we rolled our hoops along the
chestnut-shaded alleys of the Champs Élysées where dignified *nourrices* in their wide cloaks and lace caps with
ribbon streamers to the knees walked, each carrying in
her arms the baby she had in charge, or stopped to nurse
it from full white breasts while the baby's mother in an
elegant dress and tight-fitting gloves watched as if she
were not truly a part of her child. We were given sticks
of *sucre d'orge* to suck into a fine point as we sat on a
bench before a puppet theater to watch Guignol with
his air of innocence and his knack of getting caught by
the ever-vigilant policeman who rapped Guignol's head
against the boards with a sharp sound which never failed
to distress the children who heard and saw. I had not,
somehow, felt as sorry for Punch when I had seen the
puppet shows at home. Sometimes we went to spin our
tops in the Tuileries, keeping them whirling with strokes
from the lash of a whip, stopping at four o'clock on
warm afternoons when our governess, Mademoiselle
Valton, who smelled of mourning weeds, bought our
goûter, slabs of chocolate and *petit pain* or brioche, from
a man who patrolled the grilled spaces, basket over his
arm. She placed us then on metal chairs, paying two

cents for their hire from a woman in a rusty black dress who fished deep into the pocket of her voluminous skirt to bring out the change. After goûter there were turns on the music-ridden carrousel where with the passion of the flung moment I tried for the gold ring, astride a hobbyhorse with mane of petrified foam. I remember my surprise as I watched the little Parisians who sat supine and docile, curls untouched by striving, their white-gloved hands holding to the bar of safety and seemingly content to fly past rings that hung like swollen raindrops waiting to fall.

As a part of that faraway Paris, there is the image which persists of the ever-active knitting needles of Mademoiselle Valton intent upon the progress of a partly finished sock, as she sat on a bench of the echoing gallery in the Louvre on rainy afternoons while we three children wandered in and out of the *Salon Carré* among the Leonardos and the Botticellis, the pictures seeping into our pores as water seeped into the earth without. We were charmed by the bright beauty of Madame Récamier upright on her couch and we were involved for long moments with the intricacies of the battles and the treaties of Napoleon as they were spread before us in those panoramas wherein the faces of blood-soaked soldiers dying in agony and the lofty gestures of statesmen, so sure of their acts, seemed far more real than the angular woman who continued on with her drab task in the corridor, unheeding of us, her charges, as she was unheeding of pictorial glories.

Our trips to France when we were small began with the plans issued by the steamship company, the rustling paper upon which were printed, inside an ellipse that

represented the decks, the little boxes numbered as cab-
ins. Coming in from play on a dark winter afternoon,
we would find Mamma at the fireside on the library
sofa, beneath her Chinese shawl, with the plan spread
wide on her lap.

"See here, children," she would say, and a light of
pleasure was in her eyes, "this is the cabin you will have
when we go abroad in April."

Her pencil pointed on that day to number 279 on the
C deck of the S.S. *Touraine,* and immediately we were
able to see, as if already inside, the two berths, one above
the other, a ladder in place to aid one of us in reaching
the upper, and the sofa berth beneath the porthole on the
other side of the washbasin. We looked at the diagram
of number 279 with mixed feelings. The anticipation and
excitement of the trip to Europe we shared with our
mother, but an upsurge of guilt and fear, partly pleasant,
partly unpleasant, which I felt at the thought of leaving
school at the end of the spring term, became then something acute. And for all three of us pleasure was rather
dimmed by the knowledge that we should have to bear
with a substantial degree of seasickness on the way over.
Once, when a trip had been organized by my parents
for early March in order that we might have the benefit
of the long-drawn spring in Italy, we had taken the
southern route that lasted for two weeks. On board the
S.S. *Aller* of the North German Lloyd, we had pitched
and rolled without respite during most of the fourteen
days. We lay on our backs unable to eat, unable to read,
talking wanly from berth to berth, now and then singing
the songs that cheered us most. My brother Durant, the
most musical of the three, counted on our singing in

three parts, and our effort to hold to the correct notes, keeping strictly in tune and in time, helped us to forget how wretched we were in the heavy air of the closed cabin, our toothbrushes making rival sounds, in response to the motion of the ship, against the tooth mugs on the washstand.

We spent many summers in France. It was the place where my mother was happiest. Perhaps she was drawn to it naturally owing to her Huguenot background. Her name before she married my father was Durant, a French name by no means unusual but one I was early taught to look upon with respect because of the motto that underlies a wounded boar rampant on the family arms: *Beati qui durant,* meaning "Blessed are those who endure." Mamma assured me that it was a noble thing to endure the shocks and stabs brought by fate, to endure them with high fortitude. Later in my life, when I visited the medieval Tower of Constance at Aigues-Mortes near the Mediterranean, the fortress built by Saint Louis and later used to imprison the Protestants in the early eighteenth century, I was to find within its dark walls an example of endurance that went beyond the courage of most men.

On the day of our visit to the Fortress we were guided through in the heat of noon by the small daughter of the guardian, who at that moment was eating his lunch in the punctual and undisturbed way belonging to this class of Frenchmen. The little girl had learned the lesson of guiding by rote and was therefore able to recite the history of each cell we visited.

"Ici fut emprisonné Richard Coeur de Lion," she said as we entered a dark enclosure of dripping walls where

my heart went out to bold Richard the Lionhearted and the sufferings laid upon him here. In other cells she spoke the names of the various crusading knights who had occupied them, and finally, at the head of descending steps, roughhewn, she stopped us before the entrance to a cell lighted from a narrow slit beneath the ceiling and so small as to have contained no more than a pallet and chair.

"*Ici fut emprisonnée Mademoiselle Durant,*" the child said, and her words seemed to be enlivened with a note of pity, I thought.

"Why was Mademoiselle Durant imprisoned here?" I asked quickly.

"*Ah, Madame, elle souffrait à cause de sa religion,*" the child answered.

The story in the annals of the Huguenots was that a certain young girl, in helping her brother to escape across the Mediterranean previous to the Massacre of St. Bartholomew, had been caught and imprisoned at Aigues-Mortes and had lived for thirty-eight years in the cell shown us by the guardian's daughter. Every year she was visited by a delegation of Roman Catholics who promised her deliverance if she would adopt as her own the one true faith. Every year she refused. And embedded high in the wall below the window was still to be found the word "*Résistez,*" traced, it is said, by Mademoiselle Durant's finger as, over and over on each of the long days of her incarceration, painfully she pressed the letters into the stone.

My mother's spontaneous feeling for the French people led her to them as often as might be. She took us children with her, removing us from school at home in order that we might absorb the French language with fluency and the correct accent and that I might gain from my study of the violin among musicians who taught with thoroughness and skill. It was to Paris, usually, that we first went, waiting there until my doctor father could arrange to leave his nose and throat patients and their swollen adenoids and tonsils, postponing his attentions to them until September in order to join us during July and August in the French countryside. Then he and Mamma were apt to go off on a trip of a week or so together, leaving us behind in some spot where they believed we would be safe and happy. We were not completely happy when this occurred, for the places chosen and the people who had temporary charge of us possessed a point of view quite foreign to our upbringing.

Once we were placed at a school called Dieudonne outside Paris in a château standing within a wide park. The weather was very warm, and a dead quality in the air seemed to take away the feeling of liveliness that buoyed me when I was at home at East Hampton on the wild, long shore of our sea. I remember that at Dieudonne, during the evenings before we went to bed, we were now and then expected to act in charades, using French as our language, and that Durant, who was five or six years old, took the part of a dog, crawling over the floor and licking the hands of those who stooped to pat him. He did this very well and was the favorite of the audience. Perhaps this was because he loved our black spaniel, Charcoal, at home. The two were great friends and were constantly together. In fact, I had heard Mamma say that Durant had cut his baby teeth on Charcoal's nose. We could not have studied very hard at Dieudonne for I have no memory of learning from the book of French history, given us elsewhere, which opens with the words: "All Gaul is divided into three parts." Instead, we were taught to make flowers of paper in the semblance of roses, sitting outdoors at a big trestle table, curving the colored paper petals with a knife to form the garlands that would presently orna- ment the façade of the château in celebration of the *Quatorze Juillet* while Chinese lanterns swung from the trees of the park. We Rices did not care very much for the French holiday by comparison with our own July Fourth at home, with the sharply sputtering firecrackers by day and the wonderful rockets and pinwheels at eve- ning.

On another one of their trips, when I was nearing ten, our parents left us at Moret-sur-Loing, a small ancient town on the borders of the Fontainebleau forest. We stayed at the Hôtel du Cheval Noir with Mademoiselle Valton to look after us and tell us to behave. Each after- noon we went out in a donkey cart, taking turns at driv- ing when once we were safely beneath the great forest trees where no rattling carts with their whip-driven horses and but few carriages came. We stopped the don- key, tying the docile beast to a tree, when we reached the clearing where under a hot sun blackberries grew in profusion on sprawling bushes. The fruit was deli- cious, the berries black and large as the beads of jet that hung from Mademoiselle Valton's neck. When Sunday came, we children had our first taste of the Roman Catholic liturgy as we accompanied our devout Made- moiselle into the venerable church to kneel with her upon the cold pavement at the procession of the Host, to breathe the incense and to eat the holy bread, which tasted much like the brioches we had for our goûter, passed to us by a small, red-robed acolyte with slick hair and clumping boots.

Back at the Cheval Noir, we watched the preparations for wedding parties in the hotel banquet hall where the waiter, collarless and in his shirt sleeves, assisted by the chambermaid and, now and then, by the landlord himself, set china and glass and silver upon the long, white-clothed table, folding damask napkins, at each plate, in the semblance of cornucopias. When the marriage banquet took place in the afternoon, we children were able to see a good deal of what went on, standing near the door that opened and closed with the entrance of the succulent dishes prepared by the elderly chef, whose bald spot was concealed beneath his towering cap. At the moments of unobstructed vision we watched the *mariée* in her white dress, veil thrown back, bouquet tossed onto the table, who sat shyly beside the groom receiving alternately sips of wine from the glass he held to her lips and the kisses he placed upon them, kisses of such fervor and so prolonged that I wondered how they could ever end. After the sounds of laughter, the shouting and the clapping had become so strident as to shut out all other sounds, even the persistent rumbling of drays on the cobblestones without and the sharp snapping of drivers' whips, our Mademoiselle summoned us from the fine vantage point we had found and took us off toward the river for a walk. It was hard to leave the festivities and the beautiful bride to whom I had already given my allegiance, but the walk to the river was the one we enjoyed most. Here, close to the bridge, was the small shop which sold fishing rods and tackle and tobacco and other things that men needed to embellish the life that beckoned them from their daily employment. The shop also sold barley sugar candy, luscious drops that melted, quite literally, in our mouths.

On the bridge, we watched the never-ending task of those who occupied themselves in persuading the fish to rise out of the river Loing and onto hooks dangling from lines suspended over the bridge parapet. The lines hung seemingly motionless all day, and my first lesson in patience was learned here where man and time somehow became confused with the quiet flow of water, with the gentle motion of willow branches along the borders of the stream, with the circumspect movement of great white clouds traveling in measured dignity beneath the blue.

Flanking the tobacconist was the barber whose shop was almost upon the bridge. He was a man proficient in trimming and curling gentlemen's mustachios, and his shelves were lined with jars of *pommade* and sweet-scented, oily lotions. For the curling he heated a pair of irons over an alcohol lamp, and he flourished the metal handles with the sound and skill of a drummer at work with his sticks.

"But come, *les enfants*. Come, Gladys and Marguerite," Mademoiselle Valton cried out to us, her unwilling charges, on the morning of the day we expected the return of our parents from their bicycle trip in the valley of the Loire.

"We must be quick. *Monsieur le docteur* and *Madame* your mother can arrive at any moment." And she seized a hand of each girl, one on either side of her. Durant stood a little apart before the entrance to the hotel, a grin of reminiscent interest on his face, his eyes deep in reflection. He had been witness to more than one battle between his sisters and Valton. These rarely concerned him because, being a boy, he was less in contact than we with our governess, less regimented, and because his nature was less rebellious than ours.

The battle on that particular morning concerned Marjory and me for the reason that Mademoiselle Valton wished to take us to the town barber that he might use his curling irons on our hair. To this we were much opposed. Not only was the *coiffeur* chiefly a purveyor to men, but we had already experienced the unpleasant pull of his irons, the odor of burning hair. Also we realized that Mademoiselle took us to the coiffeur, who frizzed our heads until we looked like the illustration of Fiji Islanders in our geography book, so as to escape having to roll our hair on curl papers at night as Mamma had expected her to do. We resisted with all our might, therefore, giving in at last only because of the picture she drew of our father's disappointment in having on his return to embrace his two darlings, *"ses deux petites chéries,"* with their hair lank and dispirited.

Our parents arrived, I remember, just before suppertime, dismounting from the hired tandem bicycle as if taking leave of an old friend. While Papa unfastened the knapsacks and led the bicycle around to the rear alley, Mamma came forward to where we children waited, hanging back a little, rather shy of the parents we had not seen for so long, unused to our mother as she appeared in her bicycling costume, full bloomers and long black stockings beneath the boned blouse and high collar of everyday and a cap with visor fore and aft.

"Well, darlings, how are you?" She stooped to kiss Durant, then moved toward Marjory and me.

"All right, I guess," we answered.

"But, *les enfants,* where are your manners?" Mademoiselle asked as she put on her brisk smile. "Tell your maman that you are very well indeed, that you are *enchantés* to see her once more."

"Did you have a good time?" I asked, unheeding of Valton.

"Oh, a very good time. It was lovely! I want to tell you all about it later on. We went through such beautiful country, straight level roads shaded by poplars, and we stopped at small inns along the way. Delicious food, and the inn people were very good to us, especially when I had one of my migraines, and your father enjoyed prescribing for the children when they looked sickly."

Mamma took off her bicycling hat and ran her fingers through her hair. Mademoiselle sprang forward and reached for the hat which Mamma handed her.

"I think I go now and put this in your room, Madame Rice. The children I leave to you."

"Very well. Thank you, Mademoiselle," said Mamma. And we went to Mamma's room to watch her take off her bloomers and pull on a skirt which I thought much more becoming.

"Did the châteaux have dungeons where the prisoners were put to die?" Marjory asked. Her heart was so warm that she had been brooding about these dungeons ever since Mademoiselle had described them and the sufferings of the poor souls within.

"Years ago," Mamma answered, "captives were imprisoned in this way, dear. But men are kinder today." She spoke gently and stroked Marjory's dark hair. "We saw only one dungeon, at Chinon, a ruin now. That was where the French king kept Jeanne d'Arc shut away for a time." Mamma did not say that Jeanne d'Arc had later been burned at the stake, but I knew this.

"Tell us about the most beautiful château of all, Mamma," I begged.

"Not easy to choose just one," she answered as my father came into the room to take off his jacket and comb his hair and pour water into the basin to wash his hands.

"Run along now, children," he said, "and have your supper. Your mother and I will tell you all you want to know before bedtime."

"Yes, Gladys," Mamma said as we moved unwillingly toward the door, "I'll try later to describe Azay-le-Rideau. It's probably the most beautiful of the Touraine châteaux with its lovely light-colored stone and the white swans that swim in the moat surrounding it."

I went toward the dining room, moving slowly, and there lodged in my mind a promised land wherein were swans proudly swimming, necks curved high while they guarded the approaches to a splendid, lofty castle whose towers reached almost to the sky. And I had not forgotten my mother's story when, in after years, I visited Azay-le-Rideau, bicycling over at sunset along the country road leading to it from the house of Jo Davidson, the sculptor, the Manoir de Becheron, at Saché in Touraine where I was staying. The dying sun brought a golden tone to the delicate façade and illumined the green of the park where the castle sat petrified in beauty. It was as lovely as the dream I had for so long carried with me.

A winter in Paris when I was fifteen brought hours of scales and double-stops and bowing exercises upon the strings of my violin in the flat I shared with my mother on a cobbled square off the rue Washington where heavy wool curtains edged with fringe, and carpets nailed from wall to wall, muffled the sound of the instrument and made difficult the soaring tone for which I strove. A brief respite from work came at noon when our scurrying elderly *bonne,* lean and tiny as a tin soldier, served lunch, setting before us the *omelettes aux fines herbes,* the long loaf of bread and the Gruyère cheese she had that morning brought from market in her string bag. At evening I lay flat on my back on the Turkish rug covering the parlor divan, head propped against a maroon velvet cushion, as I read the novels of Balzac or the stirring tale of Pierre Loti's *Madame Chrysanthème.*

On two afternoons during the week I was taken to the house of Mademoiselle Suzanne Avril, member of the company of the great actress, Madame Réjane, to be given exercises in French diction. I sat in her garden, my feet on the white gravel, my hands clasped above the green metal table, my back very straight against the bands of a chair, while I recited from memory the poems of the French Olympians and tried to bring the required amount of veracity into my gesture, ardor into my voice. It was not easy to please my accomplished instructress, whose smart clothes gave off a perfume of musk and whose bearing was full of easy assurance. I often failed for the reason, she said, that Americans were apt to be cold in their emotions, passive. She seemed not to real-

ize that a girl of fifteen might be too shy, too inexperi-
enced in the matter, to bring the fullness of abandon to
the utterances of secret love. So she sat displeased at
my side, feeding chocolate drops to a pug dog who made
wheezing noises as I tried and tried again to bring the
fervor she demanded to the lines of Victor Hugo:

> *L'amante s'en alla dans l'ombre avec l'amant*
> *Et, troublés comme on l'est en songe, vaguement,*
> *Ils sentaient par degrés se mêler à leurs âmes,*
> *A leurs discours secrets, leurs regards de flamme....*

And so on into a situation that brought fulfillment of
passion to the lovers and a burning discomfort to me.

On Sundays we made trips in the plodding *Bateaux
Mouches* down the Seine and up again following a
morning spent beneath the mighty vibration of the organ in the church of St. Sulpice or with the throngs
that gathered beneath the vaults of Notre Dame, or
within the ancient gray wall of St. Germain des Près.
Also on occasional Sunday afternoons I listened to the
concerts given by the Lamoureux orchestra, where in
a crowded house I occupied a seat called a *strapontin,* let
down for the occasion into an aisle. Next me in one of
the regular seats, Sunday after Sunday, sat another
American girl who became my friend, a girl so tall and
slim that the bold Parisian men tossed remarks to her
as she passed: *"Voyez moi la botte d'asperges!" "Voici
la Tour Eiffel qui se promène!"* They uttered these
phrases not intending to be uncivil but rather because
of the pleasure the French take in a penetrating joke
cleverly expressed.

When I became a young lady, my mother and I were

alone for a time in a small house on the Left Bank that opened onto a garden. Our neighbors were the poets and painters and others who strove in the battle of the arts and the soul.

Here the glamorous Madame Réjane and her daughter Germaine, who was not far from my age, came to drink tea with us one spring afternoon when Mamma and I had decorated our rooms in their honor with lofty branches of mimosa and the flowering crab. Here, too, I worked many hours each day on my violin and my study of the French language. Memories of these difficult exertions blend with remembered pleasures, pleasure in wearing a Sunday dress of embroidered white net and a wide-brimmed straw hat trimmed with swan's wings, pleasure in the attentions of a young architect who brought me bouquets of lily-of-the-valley and carried me off to lunch at St. Cloud or Versailles and, from the bookstalls along the quais, made me presents of ancient picture books bound in vellum.

But most of all, during those months of being seventeen in Paris, while the horse chestnuts bloomed on the Champs Élysées and the acacias dropped their sweet sticky blossoms on the avenues of the Bois de Boulogne, I remember the plaintive sound of Debussy's opera, *Pelléas and Mélisande,* wherein love and longing and despair seemed for all eternity to be set down in music that devoured the spirit with its consuming sadness. When Mélisande cried, "Pelléas, Pelléas," and the orchestra supported her song in a kind of tragic majesty, I thought my heart would break. And later when I was told of the unfeeling manner in which the first-night audience responded to the music, of the hisses and catcalls that greeted the finale, of the composer's unhappy all-night drive in a slow, horse-drawn cab along the silent alleys of the Bois, it seemed to me that sorrow had no end.

Other years in France, years of marriage, varied the scene. There were summers on the Normandy coast and a winter in a great Paris house that overlooked the Palais de l'Élysée. This was the elegant world of luncheons at the Ritz, of dresses from the ateliers of the Place Vendôme, of parties with ambassadors and visits to the owners of the châteaux of history when, driving forth of an afternoon, a fragrant Malmaison carnation pinned to my dress, I felt I might have been another Empress Eugénie on her way to the Arc de Triomphe.

Such are the varied and unending insinuations of France, of Paris, gentle, wafting pressures that whisper of tradition and the beauty of the long past, that whisper of one's own past which began there with the rolling of a hoop along the alleys of the Champs Élysées beneath the chestnuts in flower.

3

BOB-WHITE

THE sound of the piano drifted upward through the open casement, and I realized as I lay between the sheets of my tall four-poster bed that I had heard the sound for some time although not consciously listening because I was half asleep and did not want to wake all the way. How delicious to lie sheltered and still while the breeze brought the odor of the sea and curled the tips of my hair along the pillow, how delicious to give in to bliss before the inevitable moment of rising, bare feet on the floor sprinkled over with sand from last night's shoes, sand collected on our beach picnic last evening. A quite perfect picnic that had been, the long August afterglow streaking the sky with vermilion, the moon broadly moving to its place above the horizon and below, our own fire of driftwood, the flames shot with color. At the heart of the fire lay an immense bluefish wrapped in seaweed and, beside it, all the corn it was possible for us to eat. Later, taking our places about the fire, full of the well-being which we Rices always felt at East Hampton as nowhere else, we lay along the sand, our faces lit by the burning embers, and listened as Papa recited his favorite poems of Kipling.

The music came from the living room below, the widely spaced, broad-beamed, beautiful room of our East Hampton house, its French windows opening on a small walled garden two steps down. The garden was more romantic, with its softly dripping fountain, than any setting for a play could ever be, a place smelling of lavender and verbena under the sunshine and heavy with mysterious shadows on moonlit nights. And from the top of the low wall, our legs dangling, it was a perfect spot at sunset for us children, tired after the long day, to listen to the music, as I lazily listened now, made by our friend Tommy Safford. From my bedroom this morning the sounds were brisk and urgent, scales running up in order that they might run down, arpeggios light and limpid as water freshly flowing. There was nothing to interrupt it save, now and then, the call of the bob-white, a bird that had small regard for any music but its own. Tommy would continue thus, I knew, chastening his fingers, obliging them to perform along the keyboard of our upright Mason & Hamlin until the morning task was ended. Even though these summer days with us here by the sea constituted his vacation from the church organ at St. George's in New York, Tommy did not spare himself. But presently the first exercises, like the daily drill executed by soldiers, would end, and then he could permit himself to slip into the music he loved to play, music carrying him so near to celestial spheres that the earth he inhabited, the earth on which stood the legs of the piano, ceased to exist.

He might, this morning, play long passages from Dvořák's "New World" symphony, making the plaintive melody of the slow movement into a tender, simple thing, note upon note almost as a child would have sung it. Or else he might choose to play excerpts from *Aïda,* from the martial music that accompanies the triumphal return of Radamès. When Tommy reached this part he would, I knew, bring out the rhythm of the march in majestic fashion, the volume of sound increasing by degrees to make the pulse of those who listened beat higher and higher. And the trumpet he would imitate by singing from one side of his mouth with a kind of blowing noise while now and then he raised an arm high in the air to beat the time with a circular motion as if a great orchestra were his to command. It was very stirring.

The "Waldstein" sonata of Beethoven Tommy played with another sort of love from the one he bestowed upon pieces of orchestral origin. Here he was precise, restrained, his fingers exact and delicate upon the keys, and, hearing the crisp notes, one following another in obedient order, I thought of the symbols in my book of school algebra, neatly organized, each in its place. And then I remembered the tales that Tommy liked to tell us of his father who had been professor of mathematics at Williams College and who, when his mind was lost to some problem in calculus, became as forgetful of the world as was Tommy at the piano keyboard. Professor Safford, on mornings of deep inner concentration, dressed himself early, there in Williamstown in the cold air of a Massachusetts winter, and after breakfast set out to walk to his classes at the college. But, as he went, unmindful of all save the unsolved problem in his mind,

the careful citizens whom he passed on his way whispered to one another that Professor Safford had not remembered to put on his necktie.

In New York Tommy held the position of organist
at St. George's in Stuyvesant Square, a place where a
mighty volume of sound from organ pipes and the voices
of a full choir were needed to fill the soaring vaults.
Here the Negro Burleigh sang with the others, now and
then sending up his voice alone in a lamenting spiritual
that brought joy combined with a haunting sorrow to
us who heard. He and Tommy, at the organ, were a unit
of heart and mind that seemed so intended by the Lord
whom they celebrated. And many who came to make
their peace with their own souls were transported by
the lovely sound into spaces that they had not before
known.

Once in a while, on a Saturday morning, Tommy had
allowed me to meet him at St. George's. On my roller
skates I hastened from our house on Irving Place to
the church, and, leaving the skates in a far corner of the
vestibule, I moved softly along a side aisle to reach him
as he sat at the organ. Without pausing in the music he
played, he gave me a signal to sit beside him on the
bench, and for long moments, then, I became a part of
the mighty labor necessary to drawing forth the full
sound of the pipes, the pressure of feet on the pedals
below, the pulling out of stops, the wide travel of fingers along the keyboard.

There was a lighter side to Tommy's dealing with
music as when he sang to us those portions of *Alice in
Wonderland* and *Through the Looking Glass* for which
he had composed melodies: the "Whiting and the Snail,"

"Father William" and the "Jabberwocky," our favorite because of the way Tommy managed to make the music match the foolish words. There were also the humorous recitations that delighted Mamma and her friends: "The Returned Missionary," a parody about a gentle old man who had spent years of his life among the savages of Africa and had succeeded at last in converting the small girl who came each morning to bring him and his wife the daily supply of milk. Another was entitled "Grant," one that we children especially enjoyed. It began, "Grant, seated at his tent one day when a drummerboy—." This was in imitation of a piece recited at a school graduation and we thought it very funny. At the end, when the drummerboy pointed to the distance and said, "Grant, yon fort must be took," we laughed our loudest.

Lying in my bed, lazily listening to the music below, I thought of these things, and I looked on into the far years when I should have become a famous violinist appearing before a large audience in some great hall while Tommy Safford played my accompaniments. How pleased he would be with the tumultuous applause that fell upon the finale as we took our bows, hand in hand. But this was a long way ahead, and I could not hope to reach such a point if I did not get up early in order to practice finger and bowing exercises as soon as breakfast was over, putting my whole mind upon intonation and accuracy as my teacher demanded, permitting nothing to intervene. When I was younger it was hard to stay indoors to practice scales which so often could not be made to remain in tune, particularly on lovely summer days when birds darted gaily from tree to tree and the sound of the waves calling in a rhythmical beat matched that of my heart. Once, several years ago, I had not been able to practice for over a week because I had injured one of my fingers. This had happened at Muchmore's Pharmacy on the main street of East Hampton, when I had mistakenly thrust the forefinger of my left hand into a large metal cigar cutter standing upon the counter. A little of the tip of my finger was sliced off, and I fainted. I came to, head and shoulders on the drugstore floor, feet upraised against the counter, as Mr. Muchmore worked to restore me with aromatic spirits of ammonia. "I won't be able to practice the violin for a long time" was the happy thought I first had when I became conscious.

I was far beyond that childish stage now, of course. Actually, I wished to practice longer than ever all summer, take advantage of Tommy's presence, playing with him when his solitary routine had ended and he was ready to have me join him at the piano corner where he sat in shirt sleeves, back to the garden, his jacket and tie upon a nearby chair.

"Hello, Glad," he would call out, using the nickname he gave me. "Ready for that G-minor Schubert sonatina?"

"Yes, I'm ready," I answered. "I hope you'll think the last movement goes better than it did. I've practiced the *sautillé* passages as hard as I could."

One afternoon Ethel Barrymore came to our house to tea. She was driven over from Southampton by a gentleman admirer, and I watched their rubber-tired runabout wind slowly up our hillside, the horse glad to drop into a walk after all the miles he had traveled that afternoon along sandy roads. I stood waiting for them

halfway down the circular staircase that led to the entrance hall, looking through a casement window open
to the afternoon sun, and I was careful not to put my
head out for fear they would see me standing there. I
did not want the beautiful Ethel to think I was spying
on her and her handsome and fashionable young man.
I loved and admired her as much as it was possible to
do. I had been to see her that past winter in New York
thirteen times as the diva Madame Trentoni in *Captain
Jinks of the Horse Marines,* for my father was her doctor
and was given as many seats for the play as he wished.
He was also John Drew's doctor. John Drew was Ethel's
uncle and he lived not far from us at East Hampton. On
one morning of wild sea when the red flag of danger
flew from the bathhouse, and my sister Marjory and I
were sucked out beyond our depth in the irresistible
power of a sea puss, he saved our lives by pointing us
out, frightened and struggling, to the guard, who swam
at once to bring us ashore. "Don't hold so tight, girls,"
the guard said as he worked his way in, one of us on
either side. "Just take things easy and kick with your
legs and we'll soon be in." Lifeguards with their sleek
muscles and their ebony-burned skin have been heroes
for me ever since that day on the East Hampton beach.

On the afternoon of Ethel Barrymore's arrival at our
house while the sun shot its rays toward the window
where I stood watching her come ever nearer and nearer,
my heart beat almost as furiously as when I thought I
had been drowning. She entered the front hall, finally,
with her beau, while McCann, our coachman, drove the
runabout toward the stable, and I slowly left the window to go down the stairs to meet her. She put her hand,

then, on the top of my head and said, "Pure gold, pure gold," in her beautiful husky voice, and I felt that she had descended from Paradise to perform this fair act.

Later, after tea, when many people crowded our long living room and a few spilled over into the garden below the tall French windows, someone, loud enough to be heard above the roar of talk that smothered the sound of the sea, said she wished that Gladys and Tommy Safford would play a piece or two together. I glanced in swift panic at my mother and she nodded her head—a gesture, I knew, that meant finality.

"Come along, Glad." Tommy's voice was cheerful and certain, close at my side.

I was neither cheerful nor certain. I was in purgatory, or whatever the last stage before swooning may be when one's heart seems to have ceased beating and there is no soul to help.

Over in a corner, sitting against Mamma's Japanese gold screen, Ethel Barrymore turned her great dark eyes upon me while I stood, fiddle beneath my arm, bow hanging downward, waiting for Tommy to finish the introduction to an aria from Gluck's *Orpheus and Eurydice*. She thrust out a beautiful hand as though to silence those about her. How could I begin to perform for her as she had performed for me, as she performed so easily, so gracefully, for thousands of her admirers? My violin seemed to be an ingot of iron when finally I managed to lift it into position and place the bow on the strings.

Impossible to know, when the ordeal ended, what I had been able to convey to the audience on that difficult day of my mother's tea party, what I had managed to give to the lovely Ethel in return for all she had given me. I knew that my arm trembled beyond redress during the opening bars, bringing to the melody a quivering uncertainty which was not pleasant to hear. Perhaps later, as confidence returned in part, the tone had improved, had produced an agreeable impression rather than its opposite. There had been a quantity of applause at the end and Ethel Barrymore had thanked me warmly when she said good-by.

Applause was easy to come by, I reflected now, pressing my toes against one of the bedposts preliminary to rising as the sun fell upon my cheek. No matter how inadequate the performance, there was bound to be an accolade of some sort, for the sake of politeness, to greet the end. The time, for example, in Paris last year, when a friend of my family, Mrs. Julian Story, who was Emma Eames the opera singer, had asked Mamma if I would play at one of her evening parties. I had been fifteen and was studying with Professor Nadaud of the *Conservatoire* and practicing for hours each day. Mamma had accepted for me, not intending to be cruel but unable to realize—for she had never been obliged to do anything of this sort herself—what horror the idea brought in advance, how painful was the actuality.

On that evening I should never forget, in the magnificent music room of the Story house, crowded with people from the American colony of Paris, I tried hard to bring out the double stops and other difficult passages of Wieniawski's "Scherzo Tarantelle" but they did not come forth properly. My terror made of the notes a sound quite opposite to the brilliance the composer had intended. I lowered my fiddle finally, with a feeling of deep shame, but the clapping of the audience went on long beyond the limits necessary to politeness.

"They were sorry for me," I said to myself, as I had said many times before. Never again should I allow this unhappy situation to arise. I must practice assiduously in order always to stay on top of what I attempted, stamp down consuming fear.

With a leap out of bed I ran barefooted along the hall and hung over the banisters to shout at Tommy below.

"I'll be down in ten minutes," I cried. "Be sure and wait for me!"

As Tommy's fingers halted upon the keys, I heard the bob-white call again.

4

BRICK BOUNDARY

In the crowded school corridor, silent among the silent girls, I searched for a pair of eyes, enormous eyes in a pinched white face, eyes that had haunted me ever since I had seen them fixed on me from above the banister rail on the top floor. I longed to see them again but attached to the body they belonged to. Then, perhaps, I might be able to forget them.

The eight o'clock gong was still being beaten with savage stroke by the old stoop-shouldered porter in order to announce mail distribution. Girls wearing their evening uniforms and lace collars were coming from classrooms to join the flow toward the door of the headmistress, but I could not find the girl I looked for, the girl who was "one of the unfortunates of the *bon Dieu*." This was how Signorina Ricci, the housekeeper, had spoken of her soon after I arrived at the school on that afternoon in the autumn of 1902, the school in England where I was to spend the winter while my mother remained in Paris.

The old porter stopped beating his gong, and in the tremendous hush that dropped across the slowly moving procession, I heard a knock on the door at the far end of the corridor. The tall monitor made a sign and for a moment the girls stood motionless.

"Entrez!" a gruff, low-pitched voice called.

The door as it opened cast a shaft of light into the darkness of the corridor, and through it, one by one, the school filed into the library of the headmistress, the mysterious Mlle. Ternaud, whom I had not yet seen, of whom the others spoke in whispers.

She sat at a broad polished desk beneath a chandelier which lighted her hair, making it white as snow, accentuating her shaggy eyebrows and the wandering tiny purple veins below the surface of her cheeks. Small, cool blue eyes, color of ice where the pick has made its mark, went from one girl to the next as the column filed by, concentrating beneath a furrowed brow on some detail apparent only to her. The wide sleeves of a loose jacket had slipped back above massive elbows that rested on the desk, and her short sturdy fingers were clasped. Gas logs burned on the hearth, sending little curving flames up the chimney, and, in symmetrical position on either side, a pair of German police dogs lay, heads resting on their paws.

When the school stood in formation before her, Mlle. Ternaud rose. The dogs lifted their heads and followed her movements as she walked, heels heavily first, her stocky bulk swinging from side to side, toward a girl who stood relaxed and listless in the front row. Swiftly the headmistress's hand went beneath the girl's chin to give it an upward push.

"I had hoped, Constance, that your travels on the Continent during the summer would have taught you that a lady holds herself erect." Her voice came from her throat, loud and deep.

I saw Constance's cheeks grow pink under the sudden attack, then pale as the old woman pivoted and, with elbows spread, hewed a path between girls who ceased breathing as she came near. The dogs pulled themselves onto their haunches, ready for action.

Mlle. Ternaud reached the back of the room and I turned suddenly to find myself confronting the great black eyes that I had been trying to find. They were a part of the body they belonged to now, a frail, undergrown body, and set in an unnaturally white face above thin lips that curved waveringly at the corners in what might have been a smile but for the searing intensity of those eyes. As the headmistress's march bore down upon her, the girl's throat gulped once, her mouth curved a little more, but her eyes did not move. They were fixed on me, and the unblinking gaze held a terror too great to bear. I turned away.

"You have no reason, Simone, for expecting important letters this evening?" The words blared their way through the stillness. Simone did not speak. "This is a simple question. Answer 'yes' or 'no.'"

"No, Mlle. Ternaud." Simone's voice was a naked thing springing for cover.

"Then why, I inquire, do you remain where space is so greatly needed? From now on, I beseech you, obey the rules of tact. Good night."

The door closed softly on Simone while Mlle. Ternaud's tread took its downright course over the carpet to the desk. The dogs dropped their heads onto their paws.

"As for you, young American"—she veered and pointed a finger at me, wedged tightly in the second row —"you will learn, and the sooner the better, that the laws of civility forbid staring at that which is occurring between others. Eyes front! You will remember this? Answer, please."

"Yes, Mademoiselle. But I don't promise never to stare again. How could anyone promise that?"

There was a faint sucking sound as the girls gasped and a report like an explosion which was Mlle. Ternaud's laugh. She waved a fist three times above her head.

"*Vive la Déclaration de l'Indépendence!*" she cried. "And now for the correspondence."

From a large leather sack on the desk, the old woman dumped a sheaf of letters. She chose a few at random, carefully examining the postmark and writing, then called, "Marie Desjardins! Cynthia Prufrock! Anna Szymanowska! Sybil Crawford!"

At the same instant square and oblong-shaped envelopes, propelled by a practiced wrist, went skimming through the air like flat stones flung along the surface of the sea. The girls she had named made futile passes at them before they sank to the floor, and soon the carpet was dotted with a bright pattern of paper. When at last the sack lay empty, Mlle. Ternaud waved a hand and there was a hasty scramble to gather up letters from the floor until brusquely, as if satiated with the sight, she brought the play to an end. She snapped her fingers at the dogs, they sprang to their feet, the school drew itself erect and to attention.

"You are dismissed, all. Good night," she said.

Girls moved past the desk, bobbing curtsies to the nodding white head. I followed the others and did as they did. But I felt I was moving in a dream.

Outside, the cold air of the corridor brought me back to reality. Quickly, I pushed my way through the crowd toward Sybil Crawford, the monitor, an English girl who knew the school well.

"What a horrible old woman!"

"It doesn't take long to find that out," Sybil answered composedly.

"She's so cruel. Is she like that all the time?"

"Very nearly. A disciplinarian. Granddaughter of a Prussian army officer on one side and a French Academician on the other. She moved the school here from Versailles during the Franco-Prussian War."

"Why doesn't someone stop her from behaving that way?"

"Who's to stop her? She's the head. Does as she likes. Her character has been warped by an unhappy love affair, they say. Jilted."

"Still, that's no reason for treating that poor girl so horribly. Who is she? Signorina Ricci told me she was unfortunate when I asked, this afternoon."

"Simone Faurel. French. On charity. Mother writes novels and can't be bothered. The mother and Ternaud were at school together. There's some sort of an understanding between them about Simone. She's here all the year, winter and summer, has no holidays, receives no letters."

"Oh! The poor thing! No wonder she looks sad.

Doesn't her mother ever see her? What about the father?"

"Doesn't know who her father is, apparently."

"How simply dreadful! Where is she now, do you suppose?"

"If Ricci hasn't shoved her off to bed, she should be in the cloakroom. Goes in to hide and to memorize her lessons."

"I'm going to find her," I said. We had reached the entrance to one of the classrooms and Sybil stopped.

"Better take care," she warned. "You can't go on as you did just now at letter distribution. You'll get into trouble. Besides, it will soon be kissing time and you're not allowed to skip that."

"Kissing time?"

"One of the rules. You must kiss each girl in the school night and morning. A way of maintaining friendship, is the theory."

"Even the ones you don't like?"

"Makes no difference."

Sybil left me to go into the classroom and I set out for the front door, making my way between small groups of whispering girls who turned to look at me as I passed. At the opening to the cloakroom I paused, holding my breath. The dream sensation swept me again, the sense of being swamped by a nightmare. It had been trying to push me under ever since I reached Wimbledon Common that afternoon, ever since the porter turned the handle of the omnibus door and I leaped onto the school portico, hanging to my small round satchel while I waited for my trunk to be lifted down from the omnibus roof. I stood there for what seemed an eternity, thinking of the good-by I had earlier said that afternoon to my mother in London, wishing she were not already on her way back to Paris. I stood facing a high brick boundary wall which was all there was to see except for one old cedar of Lebanon waving sadly at me with its great saucer-shaped branches.

The nightmare had walked beside me along the cold tiles of the dark hallway and up the staircase lit by the ocher-colored glass of the window beside it, and had clung to me as I followed Signorina Ricci on her way to a damp, unlit bedroom while the eyes watched from the floor above. My schoolmates had seemed unreal too, moving through the dream as if they had forgotten it, and so did the wicked old tyrant who made the rules I had been ordered to learn by heart: rules that locked me out of my room by day and locked me in from without at night, rules that would compel me to kiss each girl and each teacher in the school morning and night, and, worst of all, a rule that placed me at the mercy of an old woman who threw at my face the letters arriving for me and held Simone a prisoner shut away in a dungeon like those of olden times.

Never would my mother have sent me here if she had known about these horrible things. Mamma believed that the Anglo-French Academy was a fine school where French teaching methods were combined with the healthful atmosphere of English country life. This was what the folder had said and what other mothers whose daughters had gone to school at Blythewood had told my mother. I remembered our talks, Mamma's and mine, about the advantages I would have at such a finishing school, I the eldest of her three children and ready, we both thought, for an opportunity of this kind. My sister Marjory was at boarding school at Farmington and my brother Durant was at Pomfret. Papa, of course, could not leave his patients during the busiest time of the year. This meant that Mamma and I would set forth by ourselves; a fine prospect, it seemed. I had never been to boarding school. I had not wanted to leave the Brearley and my classmates and my teachers there. I was deeply attached to them all. But to go to a French school in England, and so near London, was a special sort of adventure not to be tossed aside. I was homesick tonight. I had better stop thinking. Swiftly I rubbed the back of my hand across my eyes and went into the coat closet.

A gas bracket bent its crooked elbow from a far corner, sending a flickering light over the uneven surfaces of winter overcoats, a bulky hanging mass along the length of wall. Beyond, a clump of hockey sticks grew upward, a sheaf of pale stems, and umbrellas fell limp from a row of hooks above a drip pan. Curtainless windows let in the color of the black night, and the smell of fog, come from London to die over the Common, blended with the rubber of overshoes.

I stopped at the center of the room but could see nothing that was alive, nothing but the shells of living creatures, until suddenly the faint motion of two coats side by side made my heart leap wildly. The coats, I saw now, were held apart by a pair of small bony hands while two eyes peered from between them, the eyes of Simone Faurel.

"Oh, Simone, is that you?" I gulped. "Aren't you lonely in here all by yourself just with the coats?" I took a quiet, careful step toward the huddled figure as if it had been a wounded bird to be gathered in. I thought I saw Simone's lips move but could hear no sound. I went close to her and stooped over. "Won't you come with me?" I asked. "Let's go into the study where the others are." I held out my hand.

"I cannot," a low voice answered.

"Why can't you?"

Waiting for her answer, eagerly watching, I saw a sudden terror submerge her. I turned and found Signorina Ricci behind us. A long skirt hid her feet but I knew she had come in treacherously on tiptoe. She was so short that she reached barely above my shoulder. Her eyes were as sharp as her sharply pointed nose, and two tiny front teeth like a mouse's teeth protruded from beneath her upperlip. Her voice with its false note of smoothness made me shudder.

"It is not among the house rules to be in the cloakroom unless dressing for out of doors. This you will remember, Gladys Rice. Return to your companions, if you please."

"But I wanted to speak to—"

"Go at once or there will be punishment." Signorina's tone was no longer smooth.

I turned away as fast as possible to run back to the lights of the study hall where perhaps the terror and pain of what I left behind would leave me in peace.

During the long days that followed I tried to reach Simone. Morning and night, when students gathered about the big study stove and waited for the signal that set them to exchanging kisses, I sought her out. But she did not come near. Standing motionless and removed, she seemed like a mechanical toy that has run down. In the dining room I sat with my back to Simone, while, during the afternoon walks two by two beyond the brick boundary, she was always at the rear of the procession, and in the classroom she was not with us when we took part in the general droning of French Ms and Ns and recited the names of French kings and French rivers. There were glimpses to be had of her now and then in the housekeeper's room where she sat rigid in a straight-backed chair darning stockings while Ricci drank tea, and once, after dark, I saw her frail shadow on the staircase wall, candle in hand, as a ghostly arm, that of the housekeeper, pushed her upward.

That night I wrote a letter sitting cross-legged on my bedroom cot, copybook in my lap, a boot shielding the candle light from the corridor:

DARLING MAMMA,

There is a girl here who is very badly treated. She is thin and starved and her mother forgets her because she writes novels all the time and she does not even know her father. She is kept on charity and her bed is far up in the attic and the housekeeper hates her and pokes her in the ribs when she doesn't move fast enough. The girl's name is Simone Faurel and I try to make up to her at kissing times but I can't do much because they keep her away from the rest of us. So, darling Mamma, won't you come and make a great fuss about her with Mlle. Ternaud. She's a horrible, cruel old woman but you won't be

afraid of her, I know. Oh, please, please come,
Mamma. I love you.

GLADYS

P.S. Please bring some cherry ribbon for Simone's
braids.

I tore the page from my copybook, folded it and put it
under the pillow, blew out the candle and flung myself
face down waiting for sleep. I had found that the horror I felt during the first days was a true and constant
thing, that there was no use in expecting the nightmare
to drift past. It wrapped me continually in its cold mists
and it made the warm living things seem far, far away.
Even my mother seemed beyond any point where I
could reach her, touch her. But if once, by some miracle,
she came to stand face to face with Mlle. Ternaud, everything would come alive again. "Oh, let it be soon, dear
God," I whispered, then buried my face deeper in the
pillow, pressing the spot above the letter, pressing it with
all my strength to smother the sound of my sobs.

There came a day toward the middle of the term
when, standing at attention behind our chairs in the
dining hall, we heard the headmistress ring her bell and
give us the order to be seated.

"You are to listen, young ladies, to an announcement.
An unfortunate incident has occurred in our midst, an
incident bringing disgrace to the Academy with its high
standard of morals and deportment. One among us, one
in the midst of our happy family, has committed a sin
too black to recount. Sufficient is it to know that it trans-
gresses the laws of honor and that the culprit must be
punished, must suffer retribution. To this end it is neces-

sary that she be treated as one apart. She will, therefore, no longer be kissed by you. She will sit alone at table and she will at all times wear the classic fool's cap in order to mark her disgrace and to prove once again that an act of transgression is an act of stupidity. Young ladies, I point to the culprit. Look at her! Her name is Simone Faurel."

Faces turned toward the bowed head and shivering body of the small girl. The school watched while the vibration of her trembling became a slow, rhythmic motion until presently her frame shook with sobs as wide and deep as her own eyes.

At my throat I could feel the brooch throb in answer to the beat of my heart. I looked at Mlle. Ternaud and I saw a gleam of pleasure flash across her broad red face. It reminded me of the expression that came to the face of our hockey captain when the team made a goal.

"I hate you, I hate you! I hope you die soon, I hope you die soon!" I muttered over and over like a chant, not much caring whether the headmistress heard me or not.

I sat without eating, hands in my lap, until the meal came to an end and the girls filed past the chair in which Simone was huddled and so still that it seemed as though her sobs had drained all life from her body. To me as I moved slowly past it was the saddest moment of my life.

That evening, kissing Simone, against the rules, beneath her towering white fool's cap, I whispered, "Trust me, Simone. I'll get it off. You'll see. My mother is coming to help us."

Simone's eyes came alive then for the first time.

On a dark morning of heavy mists, Signorina Ricci

stood at the study door and beckoned me with a crooked little forefinger.

"A visitor awaits you, Gladys Rice, in Mlle. Ternaud's library," she said, and scuttled back along the corridor with me at her heels. I wanted to run, to fly, to burst through the study door without knocking and fling myself upon my mother, my own mother, my kind, brave mother who had come at last to help me, to set things right, to put old Ternaud in her place, to make Simone Faurel happy after so many dreadful months and years. The dark and damp of mists vanished as I went, the dreary browns and ochers of the corridor became warm and beautiful while little Ricci on ahead was an angel of mercy leading the way to the gates of Paradise.

The library door opened, and, poised on tiptoe for just one second in order to make sure, I was across the room, my arms about my mother's neck, my cheek against her cheek.

"Mamma darling! Oh, Mamma!"

My mother laughed and struggled for breath as Mlle. Ternaud rapped the desk.

"Enough. Enough, Gladys. Do you wish your mother to be suffocated? Better manners, please. Stand upright as you have been taught."

I stood upright, hands behind my back, smiling at my mother. "I knew you'd come, Mamma. I knew you would come as soon as possible after you got that letter. Did you bring the cherry ribbon?"

"What letter? What ribbon, Gladys? I've heard nothing from you with the exception of the regular weekly post card in regard to your health. It surprised and worried me, rather."

I glanced quickly at Mlle. Ternaud, and the smile in my eyes went out like the flame of a match in the wind. "But I've written you lots of letters—one terribly important—"

"We do not think it necessary to forward all the homesick compositions of the young ladies' first weeks in school, Madame."

"So that's the reason it took you so long to get here, Mamma!" I cried. "She reads our letters and destroys them if she feels like it. Sybil told me she did but I wouldn't believe it. And she tells lies too, lies about Simone—"

"Remember of whom you are speaking, Gladys Rice. That will do. A declaration of independence can go too far. Also, there is little time now for conversation. Your mother waits to carry you off."

"Yes, dear. Grandma is very ill. We must sail tomorrow."

"But, Mamma—" I took a step nearer my mother, then pulled myself up as though I were filing past the headmistress's desk after evening mail distribution. "I can't go home with you. I've got to stay here."

Mamma's eyebrows went up sharply into a point, in the way that they had when she was surprised, and she turned to Mlle. Ternaud. "What does this mean?" she asked.

The old woman shrugged her heavy shoulders and it was I who answered. "I've got to stay because of Simone Faurel."

"Who is that?"

"A French girl. She's on charity. I wrote you about her in a letter they tore up. They punish her for no reason; they're terribly unfair to her."

"This is some ridiculous fantasy of your daughter, Madame, which she would do well to dismiss from her mind."

"It's not a fantasy, Mamma, truly it's not. They're cruel to her, all the time, every day. They make her wear a fool's cap just because she stole one tiny piece of chocolate. She's so frightened and starved and she has no one but me. Sybil, the monitor, and Constance, the other English girl, don't care as much as I do. She trusts me. I told her I'd get that dunce cap off. I promised you'd help me. I can't do it if I go off and leave her, don't you see?"

My mother looked at Mlle. Ternaud, who laughed her sudden explosive laugh.

"Such a romantic, this blond child of yours, Madame. How many of these ideas go on in their heads at this age. Best not to take it seriously." She put on her frown again and turned toward me. "Now, as to the immediate, I imagine that the packing of Gladys's wardrobe has been completed. There is little time to spare."

Mamma looked at the watch she wore pinned with a fleur-de-lis over her heart.

"We have only ten minutes more," she said.

"You may go to your room, Gladys," the headmistress ordered, "and change into your travel clothes while the porter carries the heavy luggage into the cab. Good-by, Gladys." She held out her hand but I did not move.

"Run along, dear," my mother said. "We can talk the whole thing over quietly on our way to London."

"But, Mamma! It's all too fast! There's no chance to do anything, not even to say good-by. And it's going to be fifty times worse for Simone after I'm gone. There won't be anyone to care." I did not try to stop my tears now and they ran down my cheeks as fast as they chose.

"I imagine, Gladys, that your mother will not feel rewarded for her coming by this display of emotion. You will do well to cease at once."

"Come, dear," Mamma said gently, getting up from her chair and putting an arm about my shoulder. "Grandma will want to see you too, you know."

And then at last the image of my grandmother came to me clearly, she who for so long had been my friend, my true friend. She lay prostrate now, perhaps dying. Slowly, as though groping my way in my sleep, I turned toward the door. The dream sense was back more deeply than ever, the nightmare come to live with me by day and by night. What could possibly drive it away now?

The old porter slammed the cab door shut and the coachman snapped his whip into the mists. The cab started forward with a lurch and my forehead bumped the door frame. I had been looking up, straining with all my might to see a window beneath the eaves. The cab circled the driveway, and as the horse slowed at the opening in the brick boundary, the fog lifted for a moment and I had a glimpse of the school façade. I leaned far across my mother and for an instant that pulled swiftly to the vanishing point I saw a figure standing close against a pane of glass just below the gabled roof. The face was white as wax, and, cutting the white, a pair of eyes intensely black absorbed the strange light of the fog beneath a peaked paper cap that grew upward into eternity from its curving base.

"Oh, Simone, good-by!" I shouted into the unheeding

air, and I let my head drop onto my mother's lap. "She trusted me, Mamma. I promised I'd get that dunce cap off, and how can I ever do it now?"

The mists closed in against the cab windows, and my mother, gazing out above my head, could see no more than I could of the Anglo-French Academy for young ladies. The cedar of Lebanon standing beside the wall, desolate and solitary, waved an aloof farewell with its great wan branches.

5

THANKSGIVING

THE wheels of the New York Central Albany Express rolled along the rails as though these had been polished only that morning in order to remove any small surface excrescence with which weather or wind might here and there have obscured them. Sunshine pressed into the windows at the hour soon after noon, and on the west the waters of the Hudson lay wide and tranquil while on the east the autumn meadows were spread with red and gold. Sunk into my corner, a book in my lap, lazily I pretended to read, lifting my head now and then to glance right or left according to which side held the greater glory.

I was tired after the work of the past weeks at the Brearley School, in my final year, where recently, as stimulus for our minds and tonic for our will, we older girls of the upper class had been required by Miss Anne Dunn, our English teacher, to write, in addition to other labors, a daily theme. This, over a two-week period. Not an easy or simple thing to gain the approval of so meticulous and all-seeing a person, one who had become for some of us an oracle as well as a friend. So, night after night, I sat at my small student's desk with its ink-stained green baize cover, staring for inspiration, now at the plaster cast reproduction of della Robbia's Virgin and Child on the chimney breast, now at the dying coals in the grate beneath. Often the necessary inspiration failed me and then, in despair, the small alarm clock ticking its noisy way into the hours that followed upon midnight, I set down in my copybook the commonplace words which were a sad substitute for power and originality, for the glowing thing I longed to offer her whose approval controlled my present destiny.

During those two weeks of striving, weeks of purgatory, there had been occasional glimpses of light when, unbidden, as though guided by the wand of a delicate fairy, my pencil had taken temporary charge and leaped ahead into beckoning spaces. On those evenings I closed my eyes before going to sleep with the feeling of elation tied to peace that sweeps the true believer. But the morning sun into which I awakened, or mists or rain, whichever it might be, drove elation away, and there could be no peace in the soul of a girl intent on reaching a distant school before the harshly reverberating clang of the nine o'clock bell summoned her to the routine of the long day.

This, now, was repose, like the moments between the acts of a play, seated in a train that glided with the power of a giant in seven-league boots as it carried me in its arms away from New York and along the Hudson shore to Albany. Train journeys were ever a particular pleasure both in Europe and America. Here I had usually traveled on the New Haven road during the many years of making visits to my Grandmother Durant in the Berkshires. Now Grandma was dead and I should not go to Great Barrington any longer. It was sad to think of. Of course, there was always East Hampton, a place I dearly loved also, but that was only for summertime. Grandma's house was at its cosiest and best in winter, and, most important of all, there was my grandmother herself, who had understood and protected me for so long. In a way, the journey today, along an unfamiliar roadbed, was like an exploration into new facets of my character, a casting off of the last vestiges of being a girl in order to become a woman. After all, I was nearing eighteen, and in many countries, everywhere in the tropics, I should already be considered a useless old maid, failing in my duties to posterity. High time I grew up the whole way.

At Albany I would be met by a newly married friend and driven out into the country to spend Thanksgiving with her and her husband. To be sure, I could not remain passive, once arrived. I should have to entertain my friends by playing the violin as they sat over their coffee after dinner, fitting my fiddle to whatever accompanist had been provided, a good one, a poor one, trying to engage an audience untrained in the intricacies of music, overcoming difficulties of lighting and sound in dim, heavily carpeted rooms. This sort of toil had long been demanded of me, and my father and mother were happy, though in different ways, that I was able to give pleasure. Papa cared about the approval and the applause of the audience while Mamma dwelt on my gradual improvement as an artist. But how could I be sure that I gave pleasure to those who heard? Think of the wonderful tone of Ysaye's violin, for instance, the flights of the soul that impelled it. By comparison, where were my inadequate fingers and spirit?

I glanced up at the worn pigskin violin case lying on the rack beneath a stack of schoolbooks. High time I set to work on my assignment for Monday, finished my composition, the "Lone Oak," complete it, before reaching Albany. Once there, it would not be all fiddle playing, of course. I should have many pleasant moments between: sleeping late, far from the gripping hand of regulation, lingering in a luxuriously equipped bathroom, eating a breakfast of minced chicken and airy popovers, going for walks or drives along the country roads with some attractive young man, sitting at teatime about a low table while a freshly lit fire cast a glow over all.

"Your ticket, lady?" The conductor stood in the aisle, solid as fate, and I fell out of my reverie to reach for my handbag on the seat beside me. In it was an accumulation difficult to deal with, all the small things thrust in pell-mell at the last moment that morning before my hurried trip in a cab to the Grand Central Station. I searched for my ticket among pencils, powder puff, elastic bands, toothbrush still damp, and the pennies and dimes fallen from my change purse with the defective clasp.

"I'm sorry to keep you waiting," I said, and I blushed in shame and aggravation, thinking once again how stupid I was not to learn for good and all to be orderly as were those of my schoolmates whom I admired most. How did they manage to be so composed, with everything in its right place, feelings as well as objects?

"My ticket is here somewhere," I said.

"Take your time, Miss. I know how it is with you young ladies. Got a daughter myself. I always say they'd oughter cut a hole in the bottom of these ladies' bags. That's where the thing you want is certain sure to be."

"Here it is," I cried at last, handing him the small slice of cardboard. He took it without comment, punching and sliding it into place with the dexterity and satisfaction of the technician.

I sank back, relieved, into my corner. Along the river, I noticed, we were approaching the small island known as Bannerman's. Romantic this place was, but somehow sinister with its building of stone like a medieval castle, battlements and all, a kind of Bluebeard castle whose owner might be the sort of monster haunting the dreams of children, causing them to cry out sobbing in the night. Before long we would be approaching Croton and the Van Cortlandt Manor where the noble patriots of our Revolution stopped during their travels—Washington, Rochambeau, Lafayette, von Steuben—and from where, erect upon the broad veranda, the Reverend George Whitefield preached the ringing sermon that could be heard across the river.

What devotion to a cause that had been, what singleness of purpose, what certainty. How was it possible to be as sure of anything as the Reverend George Whitefield had been, sure of right and wrong as if they were the alternate black and white squares on a checkerboard? He would have dwelt on sin, the irreparable sin of the Puritans. Today, men were less positive. There was more leeway. I myself found it no easy task to recognize sin even though a year ago I had been confirmed at St.

Thomas's Church in New York, even though quite reg-
ularly on Sundays I recited on my knees the general con-
fession, declaiming the phrase, "There is no health in us."
How difficult to subscribe to that statement all the way
through. Easier to speak confidently of "having left
undone those things which we ought to have done,"
and of doing the things we should not. Plenty of these
acts, negative and positive, there had been in my life
and must continue to be, I said to myself with a sigh. I
had never, for example, lain down with a leper nor had
I, like one of Mamma's friends, helped a stranger, a drab
unromantic woman trapped by a high fever in a train
coach between New York and Tallahassee, and no doctor on board. Mamma's friend, Mrs. Taylor, had nursed
the woman, rubbing her back with alcohol from head
to foot hour after hour of the long night, dipping into
cool water the heated compresses that had lain upon
her brow.

As for the things I should not have done, two in particular stood out: allowing a French boy, Raoul Désprès,
to kiss me as we sat beneath a great elm in a meadow
in France when I was fifteen. Not just a swift stolen kiss
on his part but a prolonged kind of mutual agreement too
delicious to be interrupted or quickly brought to an end.
The other was an act of cruelty performed without due
consideration from a bold kind of self-will, cruelty toward my mother, when, as she lay ill recovering from
an operation, I left home for a house party, a weekend
of gaiety on Long Island. To be sure, my father had been
at home to help in case of need, but taken up to the
limit with his patients; our kind Irish maids were also
there to bring Mamma her trays as she lay on the

chaise longue, her small table piled with books beside her. But it was I whom she chiefly needed, a loving daughter, dependable and kind in all the small ways. This she had not had, poor Mamma. I went my own brazen way and enjoyed it from beginning to end, with tennis parties and horseback riding by day and games after dinner or "twosing" in some dim corner with an attentive beau.

What would the Lord have said to this if He had known? He would certainly have ruled that during a wanton interval such as this there was "no health in me." Health, of course, in that case did not mean physical health, the superlative sense of well-being which so often buoyed me after a long night's sleep or during the summer months at East Hampton. Moments of this sort brought the sense that nothing could restrain me from conquering the world. Not a Christian feeling either, for no one is supposed to conquer the world save Christ. The Greeks and Romans did not know this and so their empires fell, full of iniquity. Nero, seated on his hilltop, fiddling while Rome burned. If he had been a true Christian would he not have gone down among the multitude to rescue the lame and the halt and the blind?

I looked out of the window as the light suddenly diminished to the accompaniment of a great roaring sound that shook the glass pane beside me. A train from the north tore along at full speed in the opposite direction from ours. No time to examine it at leisure, to watch the passengers within, each intent on his own business, men and women whose lives were temporarily suspended in mid-air as mine was also at this moment. To be thus suspended, the weight of unrolling life removed for a time, was something more than rest and peace. It brought discovery of oneself. Vasco da Gama, Balboa and John Cabot had found oceans and a whole new continent. So, now, might I find aspects of myself not before seen, possibilities that stretched into the future, compelling and bright as the overhead sun.

Did the prisoners at Ossining, so close to me a moment ago as the train tore by, did any one of them know this kind of inner deliverance shut away behind their bars, torn apart from life as they had been for years on end? Now and then utterances of great beauty had sprung from the pen of some convict: *Pilgrim's Progress,* the *De Profundis* of Oscar Wilde, reward of the highest order for him who wrote, serenity tied to fortitude after prolonged suffering. Perhaps suffering was necessary to the creation of beautiful things. St. Jerome, whose picture we see seated in his monastic cell with a lion tamed at his feet, had a long practice in affliction. Did this mean that nothing magnificent came into being unless by way of pain that endured?

I stirred uneasily, pressing the back of my neck against the scratchy plush of the train seat, and I glanced out over meadows which seemed now to have lost their glow. The premonition of suffering, as I dwelt on it, made me uneasy. I did not want to suffer for all the splendid things I hoped to do, intended to do. The promise of these floated in the air about me and I could not let them go, no matter what the price. In school, Miss Dunn was a part of this future. At the head of the opening page in my English composition book she had written, "You stand tiptoe upon your little hill. Which way are you going to fly?" I should have to fly straight for the stars, suffering or no.

It might be that here was the place for religion, entering after periods of stress to comfort and assuage. But I
preferred to think of religion as it had so far been for me,
an enforcement of inner pleasure, a part of the best moments. These moments sprang from the thought of
things to come, were woven with thoughts of love and
marriage and delicious sacrifice for another, as also they
sprang from the happy premonition of creative work
gradually thrusting its shoots toward heaven. Already I
had had intimations of prolonged felicity, not alone in
church below a gilt and flower-laden altar, but in my
walks by moonlight at East Hampton across daisy-
strewn meadows between our house and the softly
stirring sea; seated on the floor of our New York library
below the sofa where my mother lay as she read to me
from the book of Browning's poems "The Bishop Orders His Tomb at St. Praxed's Church" or "Rabbi Ben
Ezra"; again in the Berkshires with my grandmother in
her welcoming house beneath a mountain. Here, during
many years, leaving school as I recovered from some
nagging illness, fed on corn meal and syrup and roast
beef and gravy, reading cross-legged on the seat of a
winged chair, I now and then went up the mountain,
climbing through underbrush, tearing my skirt on briers,
hanging to a tree, one foot above another when the angle
grew steep, to reach, at last, the clearing at the top, an
invitation to let my spirit soar. I looked down, then,
upon the valley, quiet save for the passing of the morning train on its northward journey, a train of elderly
dark brown cars moving with dignified deliberation,
each one slightly dislocated, like the awkward movement

of an aging spinster with arthritis in her knees. The valley remained at peace under the daily visitation, while
the smoke from the waiting engine went upward into
the sky, thus matching the direction of the steeple
mounting from the gray stone church. I loved that
small gray church. With what joy on one fine Sunday
morning I had joined the choir in singing a hymn set
to the lovely haunting music of the sixteenth century:

> My God, how wonderful Thou art,
> Thy majesty how bright!
> How beautiful Thy mercy-seat,
> In depths of burning light!

I had at that moment been a part of the company of
heaven and I had believed that I should remain a part
forever. This, of course, could not be. There was, first
of all, my own nature to deal with, its sudden out-
bursts of despair or fury, its long engagements with colorless regimentation when the spirit refused to be nourished. There were also, as deterrents, portions of the
service, those of contrition especially, that were hard to
follow all the way. I disliked the idea of an angry God
who must at all costs be propitiated lest disaster fall.
Last Sunday in New York at St. Thomas's Church I
had read the responses from the 90th Psalm, speaking
aloud the ninth verse:

> For when thou art angry all our days are gone: we
> bring our years to an end as it were a tale that is
> told.

This seemed not a credible statement, yet many people believed it. My grandfather Durant, who lived in Albany before his death, believed it with all his might. He was happiest, my grandmother told me, when, a busy grain merchant, he turned the key once a year on the office of his warehouse and, forsaking the oats, the peas and the beans, made the summer excursion to Lake Mohonk in the Catskills. There he set to work in a borrowed pulpit to warn sinners from the paths of wickedness while at the same time he attempted to appease the wrath of Jehovah in the matter of his own spiritual lapses.

Grandpa Durant had "gone to his Heavenly Father," my grandmother said, too early for the good of us children, Durant and Marjory and me. A pity we could not have remembered him as something more substantial and governing than a benign shadow, with his broad brow and his smile that curved the lips visible above the flowing red beard. But his kindness and his smile must have been obliterated at the times when he dealt with the God of fury.

It was this side of religion which had driven my mother away; it frightened and repelled her as a girl so that, although she tried to be sympathetic when I announced my decision to be confirmed, I saw her left eyebrow go up into a point on her forehead, an involuntary sign that my pronouncement went against the grain. And it was Papa who took me all the way around Central Park on that lovely afternoon in May when the confirmation service had ended, driving me in a runabout behind a swiftly moving roan cob while I sat quietly at his side, tasting my new-found bliss, breathing in the odor of lily-of-the-valley that rose from the bouquet pinned to my breast.

Mamma was wise and good even though she did not go often to church. Among the books on her reading table were one on Confucius and another on Buddha. She believed in the search for the soul, an ardent search for each of us, no matter what the form. And she believed in kindness too. The Cheeryble brothers in *Nicholas Nickleby* she was particularly fond of with their devious and funny ways of giving help. Once I overheard a conversation between Mamma and her great friend Mrs. de Kay. It had to do with Bernard Shaw, whose plays just then were beginning to appear and to delight many people.

"But, Jeannie," Mrs. de Kay exclaimed, "he pokes fun at the sanctity of the family!"

"High time someone did that," Mamma answered.

I listened as they talked and I did not entirely know which to believe. Mrs. de Kay had eight children and worked diligently at bringing them up. Not easy for her to poke fun at any of this. My mother had been conscientious as could be with us children, with what she spoke of as our "proper development" continually at heart. Yet she loved to laugh in wholehearted fashion and she disliked any show of hypocrisy. This was the reason for her great enjoyment of Bernard Shaw. I myself had just finished reading *You Never Can Tell* and I laughed as hard and long as when on Sunday evenings at East Hampton we children got the giggles and had to be sent from table.

The train slowed for the Poughkeepsie station and

above on a hill I saw the State Hospital. It was of a pleasant shade of stone and the grounds about it held lofty
trees, but a sad and desperate place it must be inside, I
thought, with its endless restraints. All those sorrowing
people. How fortunate I was, and my family and my
friends, to be out in the world, free, unhampered, able
to do the guiding for ourselves.

Free—untrammeled—such blessings I should remember to recognize before God, saying, "Thank you, dear
Lord," over and over again, making sure that he heard,
giving something back in return. For you could not take
your blessings continuously for granted, could you, as a
matter of course? Like a slot machine that keeps on
endlessly receiving people's pennies. The quiet English
poet from Dorset, William Barnes, wrote of this. I had
been shown his poem by Miss Dunn and had copied it
into my Commonplace Book:

> God wills that in a ring
>   His blessings should be sent
> From living thing to thing
>   And nowhere stayed or spent;
> And every soul that takes
>   And gives not on again
> Is so a link that breaks
>   In heaven's love-made chain.

William Barnes had counted and received his blessings
both; a country schoolmaster, a poet, a lover of the land
in which he dwelt.

I looked at my watch. Almost an hour ahead in which
to bring "The Lone Oak" to an end. I had begun it

over a year ago on my last visit to Grandma Durant, the last I would ever make, during the summer before Mamma had taken me off to the French school in England, the school where I had been so unhappy. Unhappiness had struck at me swiftly once again when, not long after our return, Grandma had died. I should no longer, as I used to do while she lived, draw a stool close beside the low Morris chair where she read the long day through, draw close in order that she might hear me when I asked a question of her. She put her book down then and smiled, glad of the interruption, glad to be brought out of solitude and into a world beyond herself. In all the years of my knowing her, she had not complained about her sweeping deafness, had rather laughed it off, sometimes mimicking in gay and gallant fashion the manners and attitudes of the rest of us when we sat, a large company, at table engaged in a conversation which she could not hear. Only the members of her family and a few intimates were able to communicate with her, those who, coming to call, placed themselves opposite her in the tête-à-tête chair, a double-seated contrivance wherein she faced the speaker close at hand. There my grandmother sat during these visits upright and attentive, holding by its handle the black rubber fan she called her dentiphone, holding it between her teeth, removing it to laugh at some quip or to make a swift retort, a business which she knew and enjoyed as repartee. I should no longer hear the stories of her youth when as a child she had been taken from her parents and her many brothers and sisters to be brought up in the house of relatives at Terryville near Bristol in Connecticut where the Terry clocks were made, the pretty, old-fashioned clocks whose wooden works were concealed by a strip of hand-painted glass depicting a landscape. Grandma often began these stories with an account of her own two grandmothers which, though brief, made a lasting picture.

"Grandmother Terry," she told me, "wore calico and swept with a broom. Grandmother Parsons wore black taffeta and sat in a rocking chair taking snuff from a box of red lacquer."

Now that Grandma would not again be at Great Barrington to welcome me, I should go for no more walks through open meadows, climbing stone walls, leaping over brooks, coming suddenly out of a dream to behold a giant tree that stood in composure before me, its wide old branches drowned in leaves, its high independence belying its years, immense as it was, superbly sure. Now this tree, out of the past, had become my subject, my problem to deal with as soon as might be while my thoughts, I hoped, would flow full and smooth like the great river below me. The story of the oak tree was to be the last of my daily themes, and I counted on its surpassing the others, not just "the best I could do" but "better than I could do," as Miss Dunn had urged.

I opened the composition book and once again I saw on the title page the words in red ink: "You stand tiptoe." What was the start of that poem as Keats had composed it?

I stood tiptoe upon a little hill,
The air was cooling, and so very still . . .

How lovely were those words! More lovely than any other words could have been for him, the poet, at that moment in time.

A moment in time. Where, oh where, was I to choose between all the fine offerings that poured down upon me, along with the unimpeded sun of a day in autumn?

6

GARDEN ADVENTURE

AT THE newsstand of the Back Bay Station in Boston, Elizabeth Hoyt asked the attendant for a package addressed to her.

"Here you are, Miss." And he handed her a neat cardboard box, square and white and tied with fine string. It was the same-sized box tied with the same string that he handed her every morning at this hour as she and I arrived to catch the 8:55 train for Forest Hills. The box had been delivered, as arranged, by a messenger from the Women's Industrial Union and it contained four sandwiches and two cupcakes with chocolate or vanilla frosting. In a green baize bag flung over my shoulder there was a thermos bottle filled with cocoa, two enamel cups and two substantial notebooks, one apiece. This was our daily equipment.

Elizabeth bought a morning paper from the obliging attendant and folded it to tuck beneath her arm, thus making of it an object as tidy as the sandwich box she was to carry. Each of her gestures was precise and tell-

ing, and I envied her the power she had of being me-
thodical, a natural attribute peculiar to her, it seemed to
me who was born without it. My gestures, by contrast
with Elizabeth's, were scattered, careless, and my appearance betrayed a hasty unconcern: the skirt of my suit
was often twisted, the front seam a little to the rear, and
a lock of hair was apt to stray from the topknot holding
it. Elizabeth, on the other hand, was always trim in her
suit of imported tweed, her dark heavy hair smoothly in
place, her hands carefully gloved. She was, however, not
in the least prim. Her large brown eyes looked out upon
the world with a wide concern that often was brushed
with the swift light of humor.

Presently, as we stood waiting, two young ladies side
by side, a man in uniform and visored cap at the station
elevator called, "Train for Roxbury, Heath, Jamaica
Plain and Forest Hills!"

He called the names with a lilting rhythm until he
reached the final word "Hills" when his voice fell three
tones to end with a prolonged kind of sadness. It seemed
to wrap those hills in mystery, to invest a pilgrimage in
their direction with a tragic air. Forest Hills at the end
of the line was our destination each morning, but when,
on leaving the train, we descended the station steps to
reach the autumn pavements of a suburban town, we
found it in no way different from other towns of its size,
and the clinging element of tragedy was soon dissipated.
In fact there were no hills of any sort visible to Elizabeth
and me as we walked carrying our bundles toward the
gate of the Arnold Arboretum, where we were to pursue
our studies of trees and shrubs, working for the status
of landscape gardener, a profession which seemed de-

lightful above all others. Neither one of us had wanted to go to college, although I had qualified in several subjects, and now, with a year or two of parties and frivolity behind us, it seemed essential to work for a career, rather than to drift aimlessly, awaiting love and marriage.

Once inside the Arboretum, we became aware of a rise in terrain which we had learned to call Bussey Hill, and beyond was another covered with ancient hemlock that grew high into the sky. Here were plantations of rhododendron, azalea and laurel set out years earlier according to the plans of Professor Charles Sargent who had been the creator and for many years the director of the Arboretum.

Professor Sargent was, to us girls, an old man now as he stumped along the Arboretum paths, tall and heavy and deliberate and impressive, leaning upon a stick. His hair was white and he wore a white beard and drooping white mustache beneath a large prominent nose, and his eyes seemed also to have a downward drooping look, one of melancholy, as though they were intent on some long-lived chagrin upon which he brooded. But the determination of his jaw and the thick-set formation of his shoulders matched the immense vigor of his energies.

We feared the all-powerful professor during the initial months of our labors at the Arboretum, blunt as he was, curt, downright, bored with any but the side of life he had chosen for his own, the side embroidered round with growing plants. Later, when I came to know him well, I found that he resembled a tree that collects about its stout trunk the climbing creeper which serves to soften aging contours, to cover knotty excrescences in bark.

The professor loved trees and shrubs and the beauty of fine plants as most men love children and grand-children or as they love a fair lady. He did not limit his allegiance to the aristocratic members of the world of flora but embraced with fondness any species suitable to the spot wherein it grew. There was, for instance, the *Rhus toxicodendron,* commonly known as poison ivy, a great favorite of the professor. "A handsome plant," he would say, pointing it out to us along the formal drive-way of his house in Brookline, as it encircled a great rock, stiffly bunched twigs bright with the glow of the dying November sun. "Needs to be properly cultivated in order to show its full worth." He might have been speaking of a child hitherto overlooked among the more brilliant members of a large family.

Indoctrinations such as this took place for us later on. As yet Elizabeth and I had not been to Holm Lea, the Sargent place off Jamaica Pond. Indeed, we barely knew Professor Sargent, having seen him at close range only on the day after our arrival in Boston when we called on him at the administration building of the Arboretum to present the letter written in our behalf by Beatrix Cadwallader Jones, a landscape gardener of note and a friend of ours in New York. In the letter she ex-plained to the professor that we two girls, then nearing twenty-one, hoped to become professional gardeners like herself, that the outset of our training meant learning the names and requirements of the hardy trees and shrubs of North America and that in no other spot save the Arboretum could this be accomplished thoroughly. She had advised us, she told him also, to begin our studies in the autumn that we might first be introduced to the trees when they were bare, thereby bringing us knowledge of their basic appearances and habits. She hoped, Beatrix Jones said, ending her letter, that the professor would deal kindly with us.

We were received in Professor Sargent's office. He stood behind a large, book-strewn table as we entered, holding to it with both hands, swaying a little in the way a deeply rooted oak sways in a slow wind. He remained standing and did not invite us to sit.

"I have a high regard for the lady who writes this letter," he said. "And so I plan to stretch a point in order to please her. We do not ordinarily provide courses in landscape gardening at the Arboretum, but I shall see which one of our staff may be able to act as docent. If you will return to this office tomorrow morning at nine-thirty wearing stout boots, prepared for a walk of several hours, I think I can promise you that your education will begin. Remember that motor cars are forbidden in the Arboretum grounds and that all exploration and study must be conducted on foot."

"Thank you, Professor Sargent," we said, elated.

His countenance did not change. There was no light in his eyes as he said, "We shall see how serious you young ladies are. Many of your sex have little knowledge of that word," and he held out his hand in good-by.

We stepped forward each in turn and I wondered how long this stern arbiter would put up with our ignorance. He seemed, as he looked down on us from above, a formidable autocrat to be appeased by nothing save perfection.

This was the beginning of our schooling, work as demanding as anything I could remember. There was not even a moment left in which to practice my violin. For the time being I was obliged to drop it entirely. We left our boardinghouse on the water side of Beacon Street, near Clarendon, after a hurried breakfast at eight-forty every morning except Sunday, to walk to the Back Bay Station and reach the Arboretum building five minutes before the appointed hour. Here we waited at the entrance until a lean man with rumpled hair and prominent Adam's apple appeared, nodded to us, said, "Good day," and asked, "You young ladies ready to start?" He asked this each day and always we said yes, we were ready. Then we turned to follow as he moved down the steps and onto the pavement leading to one of the far reaches of the grounds.

Our instructor had been introduced to us on the first working day as Mr. Jack. He walked fast without seeming effort in a loose-jointed sort of way that covered an immense amount of ground, and he wore a suit of no special shape or color and an unremarkable tie and shoes that carried dust in their creases. The thing about him that one noticed and remembered was the smile that enlivened his face when he pointed to a fine specimen of Carolina hemlock or a bright-berried viburnum or a well-formed pin oak, its drooping branches still clothed in faded leaves. Mr. Jack, like Professor Sargent and probably every person working in that large administration building, lived for and within the world of woody plants that sent their roots deep beneath the soil and their branches toward heaven. The hearts of people such as these came alive when they were in company with a tree of fine symmetry, their blood coursing in apparent harmony with its sap; an example of the psychiatrist's term "identification," only that in the case of plant lovers their devotion was deep and profound and valid and tender and lifelong in its duration. This sort of allegiance remained contagious for several years after my marriage. When the rearing of children, the hours of violin practice, the duties of wife and the cares of the house made active gardening a thing of the past, I nonetheless held to an undeviating interest in plants as well as to a continued friendship with Professor Sargent. During these later years under the professor's guidance I stocked the shelves of our library with books such as Downing's *Landscape Gardening*, with its fine wood and steel engravings, Sargent's *Manual of the Trees of North America* and, notably, the ten huge bound volumes that comprise the long defunct magazine *Garden and Forest* which Sargent edited during the nine years of its existence. An article published in this magazine on February 6, 1889, deepened my understanding of the plant devotee and his dedicated capacity for labor. Pleading for a beneficent administration of public parks, Professor Sargent wrote:

. . . The work, therefore, of the true landscape maker is essentially unselfish; he can hardly hope to witness its completion, and his only delight is that of conception and of watching its growth as far as he may; the latter activity, akin to parental responsibility, is commingled with pain. . . . It may be seen, then, that no other form of art creation deserves more reverent care, more protection from thoughtless or mischievous hands, than that of such a master whose canvas is the earth and whose pigments are

the objects themselves that the painter aims to coun-
terfeit—the turf, the trees, the grass, the flowers, the
rocks, the water, under changing skies.

I thought these words very beautiful, very moving,
and I came to be, because of them, more than ever fond
of the irascible old man who was their author and more
in sympathy with the wars he waged in the cause of
creation as this applied to the "master whose canvas is
the earth."

As a young student of arboriculture, I had a long way
to go before reaching this awareness and appreciation
and the knowledge that must precede these things. Elizabeth Hoyt and I, assiduously taught by Mr. Jack, were expected to memorize the Latin names of every plant that
had its being within the widely encircling Arboretum
walls. Thus the tree which in the past we had casually
known as the sugar maple became *Acer grandidenta-
tum,* the common lilac turned into *Syringa vulgaris* and
we were instructed to name the old-fashioned syringa or
mock-orange bush, *Philadelphus coronarius.* In addition
to the raising of the familiar to another plane, there was
all of the new and unfamiliar to make our own. On our
walks that lasted two to three hours, Mr. Jack often confronted us with plants native to China and Japan, many
of them sprung from seed gathered in those far lands by
a distinguished and exceptional member of the staff, Dr.
Ernest Wilson, worthy successor to Marco Polo, who in
the account of his own travels had spoken of seeing
"roses as big as cabbages" and "pears a foot long," thus
describing the tree peony and the fruit of the oriental
quince. Wilson, we were told, had broken a leg in his

zeal, during a stiff climb of the Himalayas as he searched for rare evergreens, and had had a most painful three-day journey down into civilization strapped to the back of a coolie. Dr. Wilson's major contribution, perhaps, sprang from the seed he gathered, on that difficult Himalayan trip, of the cedar of Lebanon which had since proved hardy in the chill climate of Massachusetts. Once introduced to the gardens of America, we were assured, it would become a year-round companion to our own native trees. I thought of the many English novels in which tea on the lawn beneath the cedars was the setting for happy events as the long twilight unfolded into tranquillity. Perhaps, in our cruder land, we might one day be blessed with a taste for this sort of old-world grace when Wilson's seed had brought forth a race of the species *Cedrus libanotica.*

Meanwhile, Elizabeth and I plodded on, taking notes as we walked our four or five miles each day. Mr. Jack left us at twelve-thirty, and we then retrieved the green baize bag and the box of sandwiches to eat our lunch in an unoccupied corner of the administration building or, when the day was fine, to sit on the grass out of doors. Now and then some minor but unpleasant occurrence broke our routine, as when the stopper fell out of the thermos bottle and drowned our notes in cocoa, but usually things went well. After a mile or so of exploring on our own, when lunch was over, we returned by train to the boardinghouse on Beacon Street to spend the evening in transferring our notes to cards for the catalogue we hoped would one day fit into our office files. Gone for the moment were soft pleasures, easy seductions: parties, beaux, music, books. All was preparation for the career ahead, for the landscape firm we were to found as Hoyt and Rice.

Another aspect of our trade was work in the greenhouse. Here we were taken in hand by an infirm elderly man named Jackson Dawson, overlord of his domain, famed for his genius in causing seed to mature, in making grafts based on unlikely material, in persuading raw cuttings to take on vigorous growth. We stood beside him at his workbench while the autumn sunshine beat through the greenhouse glass upon our heads, and watched his crooked old fingers move in magical fashion among the tiny green seedlings. It seemed like the performance of some wizened, midsummer wood elf. After a time, we watched him with affection as well, becoming very fond of old Dawson with his tobacco-stained smile, his spot-spattered clothes, his seldom-changed shirt. One of our duties at this stage was to retrieve for him the eyeglasses suspended on a cord which often slipped down the back of his neck.

"Thank you, young lady," he would say to her whose turn it happened to be. "Much obliged. My old eyes need help with these retinispora seedlings. Pretty small now, but they'll be forest trees some day."

A winter followed in New York where we attempted to master the intricacies of that branch of architecture known as "Shades and Shadows." This study required accuracy and clear thinking, and here Elizabeth far surpassed me. The rules of logic as they affected our attempts at drawing seemed to me unpleasantly rigid and bewildering. They seemed also at a great and almost incomprehensible distance from the charming pictures of gardens in flower that floated deliciously in my mind as

I looked toward the future. Elizabeth, on the contrary, was able to combine the two separate disciplines necessary to our studies, and she it was who carried the burden imposed on us by the young architectural student come down from Columbia to instruct us. I could only be happy and immensely relieved when the attic room in our New York house was finally divested of drawing tables and stools and quadrants and T squares and the moment came for our return to the wide, waterside room on Beacon Street and the daily trips to the Arboretum. This was during the final week of April when flower buds appeared on maples and early lilacs, and magnolias prepared to blossom, when our companions of the previous autumn were free, now, from the duress of winter winds and ice.

Professor Sargent was polite when we showed ourselves once again, but his apparent indifference to our presence persisted still. Going our rounds as the weeks passed, in gingham dresses and straw hats, taking turns in carrying the Scotch stalking stick upon which we occasionally sat to rest, we now and then saw the professor's car on its way along the Arboretum roads, the only car allowed within the grounds. He seemed unaware of us as he passed and I knew that he had not yet made up his mind as to the seriousness of our purpose.

During the spring session at the Arboretum, we saw less of Mr. Jack. This encouraged us to believe that we were nearing a point of increased knowledge, the point of independence. A day arrived, presently, at the beginning of a new week, when he said it might be a good idea to drop our studies in the Arboretum proper so as to visit a few of the large estates round about. "We'll begin with the Sargent place, Holm Lea," he said. "A splendid collection there. I'll drive you over in the morning." We sat in his rickety Model-T noisily making its way along the edge of Jamaica Pond until it stopped with a snort inside the gate of a well-planted avenue. Here we left the car, and another pilgrimage on foot began.

The grounds of Holm Lea were large, the plants many and varied. They ranged from magnificent great trees and shrubs to the rock plants collected in the high Alps, in the Rocky Mountains, all over the world. As we went, on and on, no one of us was conscious of the hours that rolled away. We were conscious of nothing save the wonder of that spot planted by an artist to endure in loveliness forever. But even as I whispered that word to myself, the word "forever," it became invested with the sadness that touched the name "Forest Hills" as uttered by the guard at the Back Bay Station each morning. A pity the word "forever" had been carved out for man to speak. It brought only disappointment and sorrow trailing after. For, it was borne in on me then, man could not count on forests or hills or flowers or any other fair thing to endure.

"Now what is that medium-sized tree standing alone over there, young ladies?" Mr. Jack asked briskly.

Neither of us answered for a moment, but I came hurriedly out of my dream. "It has the shape of a *Crataegus*," I said at last.

"One of the many hawthorn varieties," Elizabeth agreed.

"You're right, Miss Rice and Miss Hoyt. But you've got to know the name of the species. Especially if you should come to this place to visit Professor Sargent. He thinks a lot of the native American hawthorns or else he wouldn't have covered Peter's Hill in the Arboretum with them and made it one of the spectacles of this part of the country. That one over there"—and he flung out a sharply boned arm—"is *Crataegus nitida*. It's a native of the Mississippi Valley but doesn't object to the climate here. Grows to thirty feet. Lower branches widespread, upper branches vertical. Remember it, now."

Crataegus nitida, we wrote in our notebooks.

That evening, on the hall table of the boardinghouse, there lay a square white envelope of heavy paper addressed to Miss Elizabeth Hoyt and Miss Gladys Rice. An engraved invitation, it proved to be, for lunch with Professor and Mrs. Charles Sprague Sargent at Holm Lea on Sunday, May twenty-third, at one-thirty.

"That's next Sunday," said Elizabeth.

"The professor has decided we are serious gardeners!" I exclaimed. And I danced my way up the hushed dark stairs to our room on the second floor.

"What luck to have had Jack take us around Holm Lea today. We'll know a thing or two about the plants in case the professor should ask us."

"Perhaps Jack heard we were going to be invited," I said.

"He supposed we'd be there someday, naturally. But I doubt if the professor mentioned this coming Sunday. Besides, no one could tell in advance whether we'd accept. We might have had another engagement." And we laughed at the joke.

On Sunday we got into our best spring dresses and procured a cab to drive us to Holm Lea. I glanced at

Elizabeth as she leaned in luxury against the cab cushions and I smiled at the contrast of her present smart appearance, in brown-and-white checkerboard silk and tricorn hat, with that of her working everyday self, seated in a dirty local train of the New Haven Railroad.

"You look very nice," I said.

"You do too," she answered. "That tan nun's-veiling dress and the wheat trimming on your leghorn go well with your yellow hair. Most becoming."

"I'm glad," I said, and blushed. I loved to be given compliments but it was hard to believe in them, to believe that people meant the nice things they said. Only with my grandmother Durant had I been able to go the whole way into believing.

The front hall of the Sargent house was high of stud, darkly paneled and immensely forbidding. It was of the kind to have been ornamented with bronze statues or suits of armor or battle shields. In the large drawing room that looked out onto a terrace at the rear, several people already sat and we stood at the entrance trying not to seem shy. The professor must have been watching for us and he came forward to greet us almost at once. He seemed less formidable than in his Arboretum office, his eyes more friendly, his handshake of the kind that expresses good will. He led us to a sofa corner where Mrs. Sargent was established. She was a large broad woman with a pale face and upswept chestnut hair pinned on top of her head, and she looked as though a deep chair or sofa corner filled with cushions would fit her better than anything upright and unyielding. I later learned that she had been for some time an invalid, and I also learned that early during her marriage she had made pleasing as well as accurate illustrations of the botanical character of the North American trees for an exhibition organized by the Museum of Natural History in New York.

We took our places, presently, ten or twelve of us, around a table in a dining room which I have remembered because of the conservatory upon which it opened at the far end, the end looking out over the grounds wherein were the magnificent trees and shrubs we had studied on our walk of last Monday with Mr. Jack. It was difficult at first to be aware of the human beings at the table—even though next me sat the professor's son Robeson, who was very nice to me—when so much that was more perfect than any person stood just beyond my shoulder. Here in the conservatory, against a background of tall ferns and flowering mimosa, were azalea plants in white and pink, giant plants and ancient. Here too were white lilies and tall amaryllis striped more wonderfully than the zebra, and fine primulas from China by way of Kew in England. This bit of information about the primulas was given me by Robeson Sargent, himself a landscape gardener with a fondness for greenhouse plants. Amidst all this, standing solid and foursquare like some self-assured family possessed of wealth and security, were quantities of clivia arranged in groups to point up the whole. Magnificent flowers of scarlet or orange, they established a splendor that nothing could dim.

I managed to turn away at last, to fix my eyes on the center of the table where silver cock pheasants spread their tails between silver bonbon dishes, and to listen as my neighbor on either side carried along the conversation of a Sunday lunch party while eating the delicious food which was, in its way, as perfect as were the conservatory plants.

When lunch was over and the gentlemen, finally, had joined the ladies in the drawing room, the professor approached first Elizabeth and then me, inviting us to go out onto the terrace in order to have a view of the grounds. We girls glanced rapidly at each other and our hearts began to pound. Instinctively we sensed, as certain old people sense the coming of a thunderstorm, that we were to be confronted with danger, with a crisis requiring fortitude and calm. I had known other moments of this sort: when called upon to play my violin at a large charity concert; when faced in solitude with a Bryn Mawr entrance examination in higher mathematics, all equally undermining to serenity.

Out we went, as the company glanced at us in curiosity, Elizabeth on one side of the professor and I on the other. Later, this was to become our regular formation, when we became, for the professor, "the little girls," when his trust in us was complete. Just now, however, neither Elizabeth nor I dared to hope for anything of this sort. We were a pair of frightened children about to be flayed by a malevolent taskmaster.

Arrived on the terrace, the professor, cane in hand, pointed without preamble to a tree in the near distance, a tree thirty feet high, the lower branches widespread, upper branches vertical.

"What is that?" he inquired.

"*Crataegus nitida,*" we replied in unison, eyes front, soldiers at drill.

"What is that?" The professor's cane aimed now at a

tall evergreen farther from the house.

"*Tsuga Caroliniana,* variety *compacta.*" Again we answered together, eagerly obedient to the manual at arms.

"And that?" This time he pointed to a smaller evergreen at the back of the rock garden.

"*Sciadopitys verticillata,*" we said. "Commonly called the umbrella pine," I added.

The professor turned to glance at us. I was not certain that he smiled but I rather thought he did.

"And that, over there?" he continued, apparently delighted with the game he played.

"*Euonymus planipes,*" said Elizabeth hastily, and she seemed to be giving me the signal to answer the next question alone.

"What is the pink flowering tree there at the right?"

"*Prunus subhirtella,*" I said. "And what a beauty! I think it's my favorite among all the flowering cherries."

The professor's smile was unmistakable now. "You young ladies have done good work with Jack. Very good indeed."

And he turned to stump back across the terrace and into the drawing room.

As we moved to enter the taxi that waited outside, the professor followed us to the front door.

"Stop in at my office whenever you have a question," he said. "And I plan to take you with me to visit one or two well-planted places during the next few weeks while bloom is at its height."

"We'd enjoy that very much," Elizabeth answered with the dignity that came to her naturally.

"We'd simply love it!" I cried, forgetting dignity entirely.

Mr. Jack presented us with a summons one day soon after our lunch at Holm Lea. We were to go to Professor Sargent's office, he said, before starting on the morning rounds.

"I plan to visit the two Hunnewell places at Wellesley tomorrow in the early afternoon," the professor told us when we stood before him, "and it occurs to me that you young ladies might like to have a look at them. Among the best."

"We'd like very much to go," said Elizabeth.

"Oh, yes," I agreed.

"We will leave my office at two o'clock punctually. I shall count on you."

This was the beginning of a round of visits to handsome grounds and gardens. In Wellesley the Walter Hunnewell place reigned supreme, with its topiary work, acres of clipped evergreens overlooking a lake, and an Italian garden so perfect that it might have been set down before a gentleman's house in Verona. Close at hand was the Henry Hunnewell garden, less pretentious but equally perfect in its quiet, charming way. I could not then foresee that a few years later, as a bride in Boston, I was to spend many happy hours playing violin and piano sonatas with Mr. Henry Hunnewell's daughter Christine, brought up in this lovely spot.

Besides the awed pleasure we had in observing the wonders of this first day with the professor, there were other wonders in spots to which he took us, places that still further opened our eyes to the noble art of the gardener. At Lancaster, to the north, we visited the beautiful places belonging to the Thayer family. Here it was not difficult to see that the professor had lost his

heart in particular to the wooded walk and natural garden planted by Mrs. John Thayer. The sun, as we went
on a fine spring morning, dropped through the new
young leaves of benzoin and hornbeam to heighten the
grace of wild flowers growing in innocence at their feet.
We passed trillium and jack-in-the-pulpit, hyacinths,
Solomon's-seal and the vernal iris, pasqueflowers and the
lovely golden-slippered orchis whose name made me
think of Cinderella, primulas and the small alpine anem-
one, while spread low along the ground were the Virginia saxifrage and the star of Bethlehem—a heavenly
oasis in which the professor could feel entirely at home.
Here, also, he could be in complete rapport with his hostess, the gentle Mrs. Thayer, who was so adept in com-
posing the landscape, whose choice was unfailing in suit-
ing the plant to the spot it was to occupy, so that he might
drop for the moment his manner of the pedagogue who
instructs and commands. Elsewhere, with landowners he
considered lacking in the knowledge to deal with their
own grounds, he might behave in ruthless fashion, ruthless as the Queen of Hearts in *Alice in Wonderland*.
Then, standing immobile on some rise of land, he would
point with his cane to a tree that suffered from crowding
or from broken symmetry. "Take that out," he com-
manded, with pity toward none.

The most memorable trip we had with Professor Sargent was one that covered much ground and lasted for
two days, days of endless driving when the professor's
son Robeson acted as chauffeur and we were followed
by a second car in which were a group of enthusiastic
gardeners.

We set out early one morning from Elizabeth Hoyt's

family house on Centre Island at Oyster Bay, and our first stopping point was the place belonging to Mr. Clarence Mackay at Roslyn. The recent planting here had been in the charge of Robeson and he wanted his father to see it. Great masses of dogwood had been brought in and set beneath the trees in the park to create a splendor not unlike that surrounding a ducal palace in England or France.

"Very handsome, Robeson," his father said, as the car paused for a long moment beneath the opulent shade. I could imagine how pleased Robeson must be.

On our way to New York, the professor had a look at the Hicks nursery, an old-time spot of faithful application to the cause of growing plants. After a brief chat with the owner, who came from his office to stand beside the car, the professor gave the signal to drive on. We then crossed New York to reach the west side and, driving north, stopped finally at Fishkill Landing on the Hudson River in order to lunch at Wodenethe with Mr. and Mrs. Winthrop Sargent, who were cousins of the professor.

Wodenethe was the perfect example of a gentleman's country estate as it is illustrated in Downing's book of *Landscape Gardening,* with its grounds that spread to the borders of a great river. We stood, when lunch had ended, beneath the conifers and the beeches and the downward tilting branches of pin oak, admiring each in turn, looking up through the foliage toward the blue sky, becoming aware, as we moved from one to the other, of the river beyond grass-covered banks where little white sails punctuated its placid lengths. I wondered how any sorrow could touch him who lived here.

Professor Sargent's sense of time was boundless when he was engaged with the world of wooded plants, and, although we had many miles to go before nightfall, he was in no hurry to leave Wodenethe. We set out, therefore, far behind the scheduled hour to visit other plantations along the Hudson. At about five o'clock on that summer afternoon we arrived before the gates of the large Vanderbilt place at Hyde Park. The gates were closed but the Professor sent Robeson to demand entrance of the lodge keeper. The man obeyed, feeling the pressure, presumably, of an irresistible force, and we drove in to leave our car in front of the main entrance to the house which was at present also closed. Here the professor got down and walked at his characteristic pace, slow, steady, unperturbed, toward the rear façade of the great house that hung high above the river. We followed, his train of courtiers, a few steps behind, leaving him to show us the way to the tree he had come to visit, the tree to which he wished to pay homage.

"There it is." He pointed with his cane to a towering mass which I did not recognize, never having seen its like before. "The finest specimen of pecan north of the Mason and Dixon line." The introduction made, we stood silent in a ring about this majestic creature of wood and foliage.

A sudden interruption brought discomfort to all but the professor as a man in shirt sleeves approached, his face severe, his brow set in a frown.

"You got permission from the owners to come in here?" he asked.

There was no answer. "I'm the superintendent of this place and I have orders to keep out strangers and sightseers both, unless invited and arranged for in advance."

Still no answer from the professor, but Robeson took a step in the man's direction. The professor held up his hand and Robeson remained where he was. Deliberately, then, with immense composure, the professor handed his cane to Elizabeth who stood close by, and took out a wallet from an inner pocket, extracting a calling card.

"Here you are, my man. Have the goodness to give this to your master and mistress on their return. And congratulate them from me on their possession of this fine example of *Carya pecan.*"

No further conversation interrupted the professor's study as the superintendent joined the rest of us in paying court not alone to the pecan but, vicariously, to the professor himself.

The day was now well advanced, clouds had begun to feather the sun and we had far to go. But the professor was not dismayed, and, therefore, neither were we. Only Robeson, who must drive us onward into darkness, seemed eager not to delay further. Our objective was the Berkshire Inn at Great Barrington, Massachusetts. Someone had asked that we choose the Red Lion Inn at Stockbridge as being smaller and more agreeable, but the professor had overruled the suggestion for the reason, he said, that there were many species of the genus *Crataegus* growing in the hills about Great Barrington. He was, at the moment, compiling a comprehensive list of these, the native hawthorn, having differentiated several hundred of them, and he wished to make certain that no varieties were overlooked.

"One of the handsomest trees native to North

America." And I, quite naturally, have thought so ever since.

In the car on the long drive northward, while a steady rain all but drowned the world outside, Elizabeth and I persuaded the professor to tell us of the exploratory voyages he had made during his career. We enjoyed listening to the stories of these immensely important journeys wherein he gathered hitherto unknown data on trees, data that became invaluable to the country at large. There was the task, for example, he had been given as a young man when the government entrusted him to make a survey of our forests, a task that brought him greater knowledge of our native plants than any man had previously achieved.

These early trips had involved the hardships of pack and camp life, and we guessed it had not been easy for his companions to keep pace with one who carried vitality and courage in conspicuous presence as a Capitol building carries a flag.

Among Professor Sargent's satellites during his later trips of discovery were the Misses Catherine and Louisa Loring, unmarried, middle-aged sisters, whose devotion to the cause of horticulture was a thorough and dependable one. Their talent was especially gratifying to the professor as it concerned the preserving of leaves and flowers which later became a part of the herbarium collection at the Arboretum. On their journeys together, after a difficult day's tramp, the ladies' long skirts held above mud and brier by means of clothespins on elastic straps fastened to their belts, they labored at evening in some primitive inn or boardinghouse on plants freshly

gathered that day. Spreading their specimens along the
surface of a table, sorting and organizing with care, they
placed them between sheets of blotting paper and
strapped them inside the wooden presses which would,
at the end of the journey, be carried back to the museum
for the benefit of the dedicated botanist.

"Nice girls," the professor would say as a summary to
the tale of some joint expedition. Elizabeth and I continued to be the "little girls," each of his female subjects
in her own category. Indeed, I remained one of the little
girls long after my marriage and to the end of Professor
Sargent's life. His book, *Manual of the Trees of North
America,* is inscribed to me thus.

Of the professor's stubborn, unyielding side, we were
to have an example on the evening of the journey to the
Berkshires when, dinnerless in the rain and dark, we
took a wrong turn which landed us deep in the mud of a
seldom-traveled side road, while the gardening friends
who all day had followed us drove unwittingly on. Impossible to move the car further. We sat without speaking for long minutes while Robeson walked back to the
main road in a quest for help. At the end of half an hour
he returned soaked, his hat brim running rivulets of
water.

"There's a chap with a car out there, Father, who
agrees to drive us to the Berkshire Inn."

"Robeson," the professor asked, motionless, obdurate,
"who is this fellow?"

It did not seem to us the moment for looking into
credentials and pedigree. We knew, though, that rather
than go against native grain, working from within like
some directional signal, our professor would have re-

mained all night in the damp and discomfort of an in-
adequately protected car. Stamina such as this we none
of us possessed.

The obduracy and stamina, however, tied to a high
disposition of mind, were attributes that produced the
enduring monuments Professor Sargent was to leave
behind, a well-woven rope from which are suspended
the grandeur to be seen in forest planting, in the park-
ways of our land, along the avenues of great cities,
and in the enhanced beauty of private gardens: a far, fair
world.

For me, long after the firm of Hoyt and Rice had been
brought to an end, enjoyment of a lively kind continued
in the wake of my friendship with the professor. First,
on the summer prior to my marriage, there was the trip
to England with Elizabeth and her aunt, Mrs. Donald
Cameron, a trip that completed our studies in the gardens opened to us in each last detail through Professor
Sargent's letters. Later, several years after we were married, the professor's influence upon my husband and me
was a factor in our move away from the rocky North
Shore of Massachusetts Bay. We moved to gentle mead-
owland in the township of Topsfield where a cluster of
small white houses sat in repose above the banks of the
Ipswich River. Compelling they were in their stillness,
within an arc of great maples, a flock of white gulls
poised, as we saw them first from the lane above. The
spot, lying untenanted for years, seemed to be awaiting
him who would summon it back to life. Eventually a
larger house of whitewashed brick arose on the river-
bank to become a shelter for us and our children, but
there remained always a sense of removal that brought a

tranquil aspect to the days, and, as spring and autumn succeeded each other, shrubs were dug from the Arboretum grounds to be planted in a small nursery of our own there to await future needs: a present from the professor to our growing acres.

A packet of letters from Professor Sargent received over the years, scratched in haste with fine pen on heavy paper, some of them edged with mourning band, I have kept in a faded leather case. They remind me of his devotion to any who shared his plans, his dreams. He lived a long life, and, among other gratifications, he was able to watch in the Arnold Arboretum the metamorphosis of a worn-out farm, sapped by lengthy pasturage, as gradually it grew under his decree into a museum and park of lasting value.

Upon his coffin, carried on the shoulders of pallbearers down the aisle of the church in Brookline, grew a mass of clivia in scarlet and orange, offspring of those I had admired as a girl on my first visit to Holm Lea. Would the professor have considered this plant suitable to its present setting? Or, with a frown of annoyance, would he have ordered it back to the greenhouse whence it had come? This question I asked myself as the coffin was lowered before the altar, and I dwelt on the promise of eternity for the soul of man.

7

AN EDUCATION

THE perfume I had chosen as my own was called Amber and was distributed by the house of Babani in Paris, one known for the influence of the Orient upon its wares and for the exotic aura clinging to it. Inside its doors on the Boulevard Haussmann were to be found ornaments for the enhancement of beautiful ladies: glittering bags to be carried at evening, tea gowns of rich brocade embroidered in pearls, their sleeves of chiffon sweeping the ground.

Never before had I used perfume nor had I entertained the thought. Now, under the influence of Mrs. Donald Cameron with whom I was at present living in her house at 6, Square du Bois de Boulogne, I had unaccountably become a sophisticated young woman. The day-to-day adventure I shared with Mrs. Cameron's niece, my great friend Elizabeth Hoyt. We had, a few weeks back, arrived from England where Mrs. Cameron had taken us that we might study the gardens there, gardens which Professor Sargent had arranged for us to see. This, in order to further our plans to become professional land-scape gardeners. The idea of rigorous work, however, seemed more and more to become lusterless as the splendors and subtleties of Paris took hold of our pliable natures.

The perfume signalized this step onward, its fragrance adhering to my person in a way that astonished and delighted me. The effect upon others may have otherwise astonished, and less agreeably, for I did not spare the atomizer, pressing down upon it with the full strength of my fingers in order that the emerging spray might be continuous and its volume full.

Elizabeth was caught also in the delights of this new discovery. We agreed about the magical powers of feminine charm accruing to us through the medium of the distilled essence now on each dressing table. While I had chosen the Babani Amber, her choice was a fresh geranium scent made by Floris of Jermyn Street in London and recommended to her by Mrs. Cameron. Elizabeth was much influenced by her Aunt Lizzie, whom she admired and whose good opinion she wished to hold. We were both in dread of Mrs. Cameron's disapproval, which was rarely stated halfway. For she was a person of unlimited experience within every imaginable situation of a lofty and glamorous sort. No doors worth opening were closed to her. The world of high prestige was hers in Washington, D.C., where her salon on Lafayette Square included distinguished Europeans and such men as John Hay, Henry Cabot Lodge and Henry Adams. She visited the great houses of England and in Austria and Hungary had attended shooting weekends at the country places of the nobility, where guests were entertained at evening with dances in castle ballrooms lighted by flaming torches held in the hands of motionless flunkeys who lined the walls, their powdered peruques and scarlet, gold-braided liveries adding magnificence to the scene.

"But didn't the flunkeys get dreadfully tired, standing there hour after hour without moving? Didn't their arms ache so they could no longer bear it?" I asked Mrs. Cameron when first she told us of this glittering performance.

"It was a part of their duty not to betray their feeling," she answered. "Those were, of course, well-trained servants."

A viewpoint such as this, matter-of-fact, merciless, spread dismay in my heart and made the balance of right and wrong difficult to resolve, difficult for the reason that Mrs. Cameron was accustomed to deference in the matter of her opinions. It seemed not possible to believe her mistaken. Her pronouncements were final. She reminded me of Pallas Athena, with her steady forward gaze and unsmiling mouth and the habit she had of command. A goddess imbued with wisdom. Had Pallas Athena been imbued also with warmth of heart, I wondered? The accounts of her neglected to mention this.

The Paris house of Mrs. Cameron was set in the small square back from the pavement and was reached by a gravel path neatly bordered with ivy. It was not large but was furnished in the French manner of traditional elegance. On the entrance floor were the big salon, used chiefly for parties, and the ample dining room. There was also a library which became the background for much of our daily life. Here, the walls that interspersed the mounting bookshelves were of a soft gray, there were Louis Quinze *fauteuils* of walnut, covered in faded silk damask, and a wood-burning fireplace stood ready to give out its warmth on chilly evenings. Upstairs, the bedrooms were wide and broadly open to the light of day. We might have been in the country, so green and quiet was the outlook.

In this setting and under Aunt Lizzie's authoritative eye, Elizabeth and I guided ourselves with circumspection as we went either with her or with the proper chaperone to visit the ancient monuments of Paris, to Rambouillet, to Malmaison, to study the gardens of Lenôtre or to make purchases in the fashionable shops of the Place Vendôme. We were as far as might be, at this moment, from the average American visitor to Paris who did his sightseeing in groups on guided tours and his shopping along the facile purlieus of the rue de Rivoli. Now and then we were told to make ourselves as smart as possible in order to accompany Mrs. Cameron to the house of some highly placed French lady, there to drink tea and eat *petits fours* in a beautiful ancient *hôtel* of the Boulevard St. Germain. At moments such as this I held myself as decorously detached as possible, sipping tea from a delicate Sèvres cup, refusing a second *petit four* no matter how hungry I might have been. A tight discomfort seemed to be the setting for elegant behavior, I learned during these weeks with Elizabeth's aunt, and I thought I could hear the echoing accompaniment of this life in the timbre of her voice, in the strained and sharp quality it held as though from too long and too severe a denial of the softer pleasures.

The unvarying height of Mrs. Cameron's standards was most clearly disclosed in her conversations with Edith Wharton, a long-time companion who came often to lunch or tea. Together they talked over the events in their international world with especial stress on the manners of young Americans, a subject that held Mrs. Wharton who had for some years been away from the United States. One day, Elizabeth and I overheard her Aunt Lizzie as she described life on Bailey's Beach at Newport.

"Why, my dear, the young people actually lie—not sit, *lie*—beside each other in the sand. It curdles the blood to watch this sort of abandon."

Mrs. Wharton did not have much to say in the way of answer. She was probably too busy taking stock of what she heard, making notes for her next story.

Mrs. Cameron continued. "Now and then you see a girl who has removed her stockings entirely. Such an action began, I dare say, with an attempt to get the sand out, rolling them down for this purpose. Well, they've stayed down and doubtless will for good and all. The world, our world at home, is becoming a decidedly slipshod place. Manners everywhere appear to be disintegrating."

At evening we were sometimes taken to see a play of Racine or Molière at the *Comédie Française,* no other theater being considered suitable for the *jeunes filles* that we still were, even though, in reality, we considered ourselves grown up and entirely capable of independence. As Mrs. Cameron did not particularly enjoy listening to music, we avoided concerts and the opera. So, after dark, we remained usually at home.

During the third week of our stay in the Square du Bois, Henry Adams arrived in Paris and came at once to call on Mrs. Cameron, who was his old friend. Letters addressed to her in the course of our journey had been frequent in the morning mail and I had come to recognize as his the round hand of carefully constructed script. She herself spent hours at her desk during the week, writing to "Uncle Henry," the nickname become almost universal, caught from an ember kept aglow by his many nieces, real and fabricated.

I fell at once under his spell. I had not seen him before, had not been told of his curiously short stature, his darting forward motion like that of a small boy intent on finding what lay ahead, the rapidity combined with the inconsequence of his gesture. When he chose to rest, deep in a chair, slumped, one leg crossed above the other, he seemed momentarily to retire, to shrink as does a hibernating animal, to become almost anonymous. Only the words that he presently spoke, slowly, in the manner of a monologist who ponders his deeper meaning, and the questions of difficult answer that he put to any who listened, announced the learned scholar. His abstract utterances as well as his queries appeared only indirectly to issue from the man himself, small as he was, unimpressive as a physical being, the sharply pointed beard that he wore concealing much of his facial expression. He seemed then to have renounced his human prerogatives, shaken them off in favor of those claimed by the oracle. Yet watching him over my embroidery frame, fascinated but fearful of being singled out as an inept target for the swift thrusts of his interrogating mind, I saw that he was not unkind, caustic. Rather, he was a seeker, passionate, eager, trusting, longing to believe in the treasure he now and then found. And the smile that at moments enlivened his eyes seemed to moderate the oracle's rights to stern order.

I sat, weaving my needle in and out of the work that was encouraged by Mrs. Cameron as quieting to the spirit of a young woman in the making, and I listened to Uncle Henry as he read to us aloud, watching him intently. This attitude of consecration brought its reward, for soon I was invited to become a niece, to join the sisterhood of aspirants for his favor. Elizabeth, through her relationship to Mrs. Cameron, had automatically been made a member. I was a stranger and a less obvious candidate. As I learned, however, when Uncle Henry turned to the manuscript for the book later given the title of *Mont-Saint-Michel and Chartres,* he favored nieces as an institution. Here, in the introduction, he tells his readers that "nephews, as a social class, no longer read," whereas "nieces have been known to read in early youth." He continues, "The following pages, then, are written for nieces, or for those who are willing, for the time, to be nieces in wish." I was entirely willing to be a niece in wish, to play, "for the time," the enviable role that Alice in Wonderland played for Lewis Carroll.

Our evenings during Henry Adams's stay in Paris were to become something for long remembrance. As he read to us the story of religious architecture and its influence on the eleventh and twelfth centuries in France, I came closer to the mysteries that veil the Virgin and her child and, little by little, to the man who wrote of them, the man who, in wrapping his arms close about them, sought to solve the enigma of life itself.

He read first of the great eleventh-century church-fortress of Mont-Saint-Michel, of its quieting effect on those who saw it:

> . . . Men and women who have lived long and are tired,—who want rest,—who have done with aspirations and ambition,—whose life has been a broken arch,—feel this repose and self-restraint as they feel nothing else.

A broken arch. . . . I dropped my embroidery frame to let it lie in my lap, and I studied Uncle Henry's face for a sign of the suffering that must, I knew, lie in his heart. But I could not find a trace in the tidy, aloof aspect of the little man beneath the reading lamp.

Presently, under his guidance still, we came to the twelfth century, the century closest to his being, and to the Virgin of Chartres, his Lady of Love:

> The man who wanders into the twelfth century is lost, unless he can grow prematurely young. . . . One needs only to be old enough in order to be as young as one will.

On and on Uncle Henry continued, as though to pronounce aloud the words written with his pen brought verification of his thought. It was especially upon the Virgin, I felt, we all three felt, hearing the timbre of his voice in the hushed room, upon our Lady of Chartres, that he enjoyed dwelling, whose essence he perennially strove to touch:

> Perhaps our Lady of Chartres was known to be particularly gracious and gentle, and this may par-

tially account also for the extreme popularity of her shrine; but whatever the reason, her church was clearly intended to show only this side of her nature, and to impress it on her Son. You can see it in the grave and gracious face and attitude of the Christ, raising His hand to bless you as you enter His kingdom; . . . in the expression of majesty and mercy of the Virgin herself on her throne. . . . Wherever we find her at Chartres, and of whatever period, she is always Queen . . . always calm and commanding. She never calls for sympathy . . . she does not even altogether command, but rather accepts the voluntary, unquestioning, unhesitating, instinctive faith, love, and devotion of mankind. She will accept ours, and we have not the heart to refuse it; we have not even the right, for we are her guests.

Uncle Henry paused here to turn the pages until he should come on one more phrase:

The Church at Chartres belonged not to the people, not to the priesthood, and not to Rome; it belonged to the Virgin.

He set the sheets down. The last phrase had, for the time being, brought finality. Presently Elizabeth and I, gathering together silks, thimbles, scissors, said our good nights, spoke our thanks. Not easy to thank the author of a composition sprung straight from his heart. How select words warm enough yet sufficiently restrained? An angel's grace was needed and this we did not possess. We stood a trifle irresolute until Uncle Henry gave us his smile.

"I shall be in need of youthful companions of the feminine sort—a pair of nieces will do, since your Aunt
Lizzie has refused my invitation—when I propose driving out to Versailles tomorrow afternoon to call on Elsie
de Wolfe and Bessie Marbury. Can I count on you two
young ladies?"

"Yes, you can, Uncle Henry. Indeed you can," we
answered, holding back enthusiasm, stifling it to the
degree that was suitable to our present environment.

On the following afternoon, a Sunday, at four o'clock,
a dark, lofty *voiture de remise* stood before our door, and
Uncle Henry's voice was heard in the entrance hall. Up in
our bedroom, Elizabeth ran a long hatpin through a
Milan straw and the heavy knot of hair beneath it, while
I perched a toque trimmed with a bird's quill on the top
of my head. Then, according to our newly found rite of
spring, each sprayed herself from her perfume atomizer
and ran downstairs. Uncle Henry awaited us in his neat
black afternoon suit and he opened the front door to let
us out onto the square. Inside the big car, he placed one
of us on either side of him while the chauffeur, an elderly, circumspect man with a mustache, covered our
knees with a robe of maroon plush and closed the door.
The windows were closed also against the sharp afternoon breeze, and we drove thus onto the Avenue du
Bois, through the Porte Dauphine and toward St. Cloud.

We girls were happy, alert, but I noticed that Uncle
Henry seemed fidgety, as my mother used to call the
kind of restless behavior that annoyed her, the kind that
brought constant changes of position when we sat together.

"Are you uncomfortable, Uncle Henry?" I finally

dared ask. "Would you like to have more room?"

"Plenty of room," he answered, and he fell back into silence. Presently he spoke. "I wonder whether it would disturb you, Gladys, and you, Elizabeth, if we were to let a bit of air into the automobile. Not too much, for fear of blowing away those charming hats."

Reaching for the window strap on my side to place it in a lower hole, I saw that he drew in a long breath and I wondered whether he might be ill. I could not see Elizabeth's face to find out if she was worried too. As we began to wind up the hill that skirted the Park of St. Cloud, Uncle Henry spoke.

"May I ask the name of the scent worn by you young ladies?"

Deep in my corner, I raised an involuntary hand to quiet the blush that swept my cheek as, suddenly, I became aware of the cause of Uncle Henry's recent discomfort.

"Amber of Babani is the one Gladys uses. Mine is rose geranium from Floris in London," Elizabeth cheerfully answered, unaware of danger.

"I'm afraid we may have been using our perfume rather too freely," I added quickly.

"*Cela dépend du goût,* as the French say when they don't intend to commit themselves in matters of taste." Uncle Henry chuckled, thus informing us that he was happy in our company once again. And I had taken a new step toward the education of a lady.

The Avenue de St. Cloud brought us at last to the Parc de Versailles, and here the car turned in search of the narrow street in which Miss Marbury and Miss de Wolfe lived. Entering the house with Uncle Henry in attendance, I thought of the days when I was a small girl with my hair down my back, roller-skating past the corner at Irving Place and Seventeenth Street where these two ladies lived in the small brick house trimmed with carved wood Gothic brackets, once belonging to Washington Irving. Now and then I had seen them approaching their entrance door, Miss Marbury swinging along, short and stocky in a tailored suit and starched white collar, Miss de Wolfe slim, graceful, feminine. I remembered the photograph of Miss de Wolfe, among others of his patients, in my father's office, showing her in a lovely accordion-pleated dress, her large eyes rather sad. Papa always spoke of them in one breath as Bessie-Marbury-and-Elsie-de-Wolfe, knowing them intimately as his patients, knowing the look of their vocal cords and larynxes. Today I was to see them in another setting.

The rooms were crowded on this Sunday at-home. For a while Elizabeth and I felt rather lost among the quantities of strange people, some of whom glanced up from their teacups to stare at us, most of whom paid us no attention whatsoever. Uncle Henry was at once borne off into a corner by friends who pressed down upon him in the way that the opposite team presses hard upon the man carrying the football down the field. I saw that he wished to go free but could not. We moved slowly toward the tea table and a servant stepped forward to ask whether it should be milk or lemon. Another servant offered us cakes from a silver salver, and, as we turned to find a corner away from the jostling about us, Uncle Henry was miraculously at our side. He motioned us to follow him and with but few interruptions we were face to face with Miss de Wolfe. She looked very beautiful in a smart dress which I could tell had come from Lanvin or Vionnet or Chéruit, but her eyes had lost the sad wonder so evident in that early photograph hanging in Papa's office.

Uncle Henry introduced Miss Elizabeth Hoyt and Miss Gladys Rice and we shook hands with our hostess who seemed entirely aware of him but only half aware of us. Her glance, in the manner of a person whose party it is, kept wandering over the crowded room.

I decided to try to bring her back to us and I said, "Miss de Wolfe, I think you know my father, Dr. Rice, in New York. We live on Irving Place and Nineteenth Street."

"You're Dr. Rice's daughter?" She looked at me now with full attention. "How is he? Well, I hope."

"Yes, thank you," I answered politely.

"And you are here in Paris getting an education, I suppose." She glanced from Elizabeth and me to Uncle Henry and back again.

"We've been studying gardens in England. This is my friend, Elizabeth Hoyt. We plan to be landscape gardeners."

Miss de Wolfe smiled at Uncle Henry as though I had said something funny. Then her eyes grew distracted again. "Wait a moment, do you mind?" she asked Uncle Henry. "I'd like to have Bessie meet Dr. Rice's daughter."

Miss Marbury stood not far away and was easy to find because of her bulk and her severe clothes. Miss de Wolfe beckoned and she came to stand beside us.

"Bessie, this is a child of Dr. Rice. She and a friend have come out with Henry Adams."

I watched Uncle Henry, fearful lest he be bored having to stand there at my side. He had been taken in hand again, however, by determined admirers and for the moment our mutual responsibility was at an end.

"How is Dr. Rice?" Miss Marbury asked. "Dear Doctor!"

"I think he's very well," I said again.

"You must give him our love, Elsie's and mine, when you write." Her voice was hoarse and her manner brusque. "Never was a better, kinder man."

"Yes, do give him our love," Miss de Wolfe said. "And tell him I'd like that photograph of me in my youth. It has the date written across it. We must hide these things as we grow older, you know." She smiled and left us, and I joined Elizabeth in a period of fresh waiting.

That evening, back in the Square du Bois, we sat as usual, Elizabeth and I, over our needlework on either side of the tall reading lamp while across the room Mrs. Cameron, in a velvet tea gown, occupied her deep brocaded *fauteuil*. Uncle Henry, leaning forward in his zeal, happy to impart, read to us from what he termed the "sacred sources of M. Viollet-le-Duc." The story concerned the two spires of Chartres Cathedral and dwelt particularly on the smaller and simpler of the two, the less striking. This was perhaps, said Viollet-le-Duc, as perfect a piece of architecture as any in the world because of "the just and skilful proportion of the different parts."

Listening vaguely, as tired people do at the end of day, I hung to the words "just and skilful," repeating them over and over. How fine they were, standing there side by side, direct, without pretense. Not only as they applied to architecture but as they might describe a human being. A person having these attributes should be able to bring fair things into the world of men. Sleepily, then, I resolved never to let them slip away.

8

MOONLIGHT

I HAD NOT KNOWN, when the moment came to leave
Uncle Henry, that I should not see him again as a *jeune
fille*, that at our next meeting I should be married—
should, in fact, have three children of my own. When we
parted, toward the end of that summer in Paris, he suggested sending me a marquise ring as a badge of niece-
hood. The idea delighted me. The ring, however, had
not arrived when I wrote him of my engagement at the
beginning of autumn, when I told him I was to marry
John Saltonstall, a Bostonian. His reply to this news was
half serious, half jocose. He congratulated me on the
doubtless estimable qualities of the young man who had
persuaded me into matrimony but regretted, he said, my
removal to Boston, a city he now rarely visited, and he
gave me notice of his intention to withdraw the promise
of the ring. In Boston, he wrote, a marquise ring would
be out of place. Rings in plenty I was certain to have of
another sort. The absence of his I would not notice.
On the day this letter arrived, not long before my wed-

ding, I was alone in our small farmhouse in a New York valley at Bedford, the house which my father had bought for my mother when we children were grown, following the sale of the one at East Hampton. Mamma had gone to the village on household errands. She was driven in the Buick touring car, with its canvas top and rear entrance, by Pierre, our man of all work. His wife Marie, the other half of our French couple, had accompanied them to help with the purchases and to carry the bundles. I moved disconsolately from one room to another, aware of their changed aspect. They had lost their air of removal from the world, their customary healing quiet, and wore instead a look of expectancy, of complicity, that distorted the hitherto peaceful functions of everyday. Out in the plant-filled sunroom where Mamma went to read her books on art and philosophy, trestle tables covered with white damask had been set up, heavy now with crystal, china and silver, wedding presents of every kind, that served to dim the quality of the geraniums on the sill behind them. Above, at the head of the narrow staircase, the snug little bedrooms each with the stamp of its owner were now indiscriminately cluttered, chairs and closets filled with clothing, the trousseau of a young woman whose life was to touch wider horizons than those brought by neighboring acres.

I went to a window and looked out upon the bare limbs of maples, silent under the falling afternoon sun, upon oak leaves hanging colorless and wan, upon the small duck pond and our summer rowboat empty and neglected beneath enfolding branches of willow. The moment of sunset was near and the sky prepared a salute, gathering color as I watched. The glow, I saw, came

from without and seemed by contrast, on this day of
November, to create darkness, emptiness, within. Soon
all color would fade, the aura of lasting light withdrawn.
For what, then, were the moments of light intended, I
asked myself. Were they meant only to illumine the slow
pageant of sadness, emptiness? Was it this that Uncle
Henry had found during his years on earth and, finding,
given his soul to the Virgin to keep, placed it in her
hands? His gracious, gentle Virgin of Chartres. He
loved her as—long ago, a small girl still—I had loved
another Virgin, one made of plaster, who hung above
the mantel of my bedroom, one bought with hoarded
pennies from an Italian street vendor on Irving Place.

"Where are you, Gladys?" Mamma called from the
next room, and she paused to turn on a light. "Alone in
the dark?" she asked, coming nearer.

"Yes, I was," I said. "I'm glad you're home again. Very
glad."

"I'm sorry to be so late. A long delay at the butcher's.
Almost time for dinner, isn't it? I'll join you in the sunroom in ten minutes. Put on the lights in there, will you,
dear?" And she left me to climb the stairs to her bedroom above.

A half hour later, as we sipped our sherry before dinner, our conversation, in the age-old manner of women,
veered to the "cares of the householder," to the duties of
a bride-to-be in ordering her domain.

"I doubt if you're truly interested in recipes and cook
books, Mamma," I said. "I've never thought of you as that
sort of woman. But I suppose I should ask you a few
questions."

"I doubt if I am what you call 'that sort of woman.' On

the other hand, I've always thought good food important just as good art is important. Part of the same thing on a minor scale. You'll have to learn about it, be able to guide whoever is in charge of your kitchen, no matter how highly trained she may be. The result will be far better if you do, and the cook herself will appreciate it."

"I'm sure you're right. You're apt to be right in the long run, I've noticed. Of course our food here at home is always superlative," I said, "especially when we have a French cook like Marie. It never occurred to me, though, that you went into it so thoroughly, this copybook, full of clippings and receipts written in your own hand."

"Did you think the soufflés and the polenta *genovese* that we ate today for lunch dropped from heaven onto our dining room table?"

"I didn't think. Just took it for granted, along with the Japanese prints and the Korean pottery and the tapestries and books and all the rest."

"Well, dear, you've been absorbed in your own existence, intent on your own affairs. Also, don't forget you've kept your fiddle alive all these years. I'm glad of that. You mustn't let it lapse now, going to a new environment, a new life."

"Just the same, fiddle or no, I'm afraid I've been dreadfully selfish, self-centered." I reached for a lock of hair to twist about my forefinger: an inducement to contemplation. "Think of all the many times I've been away, the visits I've made, the trip with Mrs. Cameron, for instance, leaving you here by yourself during most of it."

"We're apt to be centered on ourselves if our lives interest us. Your father and you and I, all three, wake each morning eager for the hours ahead."

"What about Marjory and Durant? They're far less egotistical than I, aren't they?"

"They are perhaps more aware of other people's feelings. Theirs are gentle spirits." Mamma glanced at me over the top of the book she continued to hold, and she smiled.

"Gentle spirits," I murmured, and sighed. How lovely to be made so quietly, without inward commotion, the everlasting strife forgotten, taking the moments as they came—"that droppeth as the gentle rain from heaven."

I slipped my pen beneath the strap in the green morocco writing case resting on my lap and screwed the top back onto the inkwell. A stack of addressed envelopes lay on the table beside me in the sunroom, the charming room lined with windows which Mamma had caused to be raised from the ground as if by the help of Aladdin's lamp when, on a day of special omen, she was confronted with the prospect of a wedding reception in our small country house. But for this room with its flowers, its branches of laurel in copper pots, the large fireplace at one end, the book-strewn table standing behind the sofa, the two deep chairs in either sunny corner, one for Mamma, one for me—but for this new actuality, already grown familiar, and for the display of wedding presents, quantities of them, on trestle tables against the west wall, I should not have been able to believe that my forthcoming marriage was real. How detach myself from a life which was a part of my being just as was my body— the body that carried me toward dusk across the small bridge to the other side of the duck pond below the house and on up past the ancient tulip tree—its cup-shaped flower shells erect and stiff in the winter frosts—

until, through a copse of hornbeam, I came out onto the hilltop whence the setting sun spread wide its swift glories in patterns ever renewed? My arms and hands were a compelling part of this life, functioning together to create the music that issued from my violin, working to dig the holes in the meadow at the south in order to plant bulbs of jonquil and narcissus which would spring to life and loveliness when warm winds and rain once more tempered the earth. Instead, at present, hour after hour during the six weeks past, my knees upheld the morocco case as my hands were involved in writing letters of thanks for the presents that each day were brought in by Pierre from the express office at Bedford Hills. These objects—some beautiful, many conventionally unremarkable, a few downright ugly—would ornament my new life, background for the person I was about to become.

"What am I to do with all this silver?" I asked.

"Use as much of it as you like. You'll have plenty of servants to keep it polished. The pieces you don't need you can put away, save for your children when they are grown."

"Eight or ten wine coasters and a dozen or so *bonbonnières?*"

"Those you can exchange at the shops they came from."

"But we use very little silver here, Mamma. We didn't keep much out even when we lived in the New York house, and of course at East Hampton there was none of it around except for knives and forks and spoons."

"Well, you know, I've never been particularly keen on silver, unless for the eighteenth-century tankards, teapots, snuff boxes and so on. However, much of it should fit your new environment there in Boston, the kind of entertaining you are bound to do. My life here, and your father's, are far more simple."

"Papa, of course, doesn't begin to notice what there is in the way of decoration when he comes out for those hurried weekends of his. But he takes a great interest in your pottery-making, doesn't he?"

"Yes, I think he does."

"That's nice. You work so hard, you and Mr. Volkmar between you and those wonderful young Italian apprentices. You deserve all the appreciation you get. The Durant Kilns are gradually becoming famous, aren't they?"

" 'Famous' isn't quite the word. Not yet. But we're very busy. I don't remember whether I told you that we have an order for a set of the Persian blue from the woman who invented anti-kink for colored people's hair."

"No, really? She must have a great deal of taste and discrimination."

"It's the complete set for dining room table: candlesticks, center bowl, fruit and candy dishes."

"That deep blue mounted on gold stands?"

"Yes. The finest, perhaps, of our three glazes."

"I'm not sure about that. The white glaze over pink clay, with the pink showing through, is beautiful, and so is the *aubergine*. It's hard to choose. But the blue has such lovely glowing depths."

I spoke, unable then to foresee the moment on ahead, a moment that followed the first war and my mother's death when, during a time of persisting sadness, I came one autumn day on an apparition. A door opened into the dining room of my friends the Richard Cranes, and there, spread along the luncheon table, was Mamma's fine set of Persian glaze sprung originally from the small kiln at the foot of the hill near the pond below our house at Bedford. The Crane house stood on a hill overlooking the Ipswich beach in Massachusetts, and the compelling blue of the sea on that October day of bright sun was a magical background for this other blue lying before us, a blue weighted now with autumn fruit and the small turquoise grape of the Japanese vine. I stood a little apart from the others and I thought of my mother's ingenuity, of her taste, her perseverance, her gallant spirit. Then, as our hostess moved us toward the table, I put up a swift hand to wipe away a tear.

"How clever of you, Mamma," I said, as we continued to talk, she and I, in the gradually falling light, "to get the whole thing going so quickly. I remember the day, not long ago, when you told me the doctors had decided you should live here in the country to keep you away from the stresses of life. Looking ahead, you foresaw you'd be more and more alone. So you made your plans either to have a nervous breakdown or to find some job. You asked me which I advised." I smiled.

"Well, darling, I was right about being alone, wasn't I? Your father busier than ever, Marjory married, Durant at Harvard and now you, going off to Boston."

"Never mind," I said in a rush of words. "I'm coming back often to stay with you. And before long you'll have your grandchildren around. And there's such a lot for you to attend to here: Volkmar's house to finish, the Italian boys to supervise, new designs to make for the pottery and on top of all this, sitting up half the night to watch the kiln, with the excitement of opening it to find what success you've had in the baking, how many prime pieces come out, how many must be sold as seconds."

"That's true. But I'm going to miss you, Gladys."

"I'm going to miss you, Mamma—and all that goes with you." I reached out and took my mother's hand, holding it for a moment. "We have to go on exploring whatever lies ahead in the distance, don't we?" I asked. "Even though it may be very different from what we leave behind. We can't turn our backs, shut doors that open for us, can we?"

"*You* most certainly can't, dear."

"Even though there's been a great deal that we loved and wanted to hold before the last door opened?"

"Even then," my mother said, she who had given me so much for so long.

From the distance came the sound of voices in the kitchen and the smell of warm pastry. Pierre appeared on the threshold of the sunroom to say, *"Le diner sera servi dans un quart d'heure, Madame."*

This was the signal to ready ourselves for the evening meal. Marie did not like to serve her food either over-cooked or cold. Tonight Pierre added, "We shall have pigeon pie *spécialement* for Mademoiselle." Pierre was proud of his recently found English. And I was touched at the baking of my favorite dish on this my last evening at home.

The moon, that night, came in through the wide open-ing of the casement window. It made its own way, oblivi-ous of obstacles, across the foot of my bed, lighting the carving on one of the newel posts to fall along the surface of the floor until it touched the deal writing table. Under its luminous radiation the procession of figures in the Fra Lippo Lippi reproduction above the table seemed roused out of long inaction and the gilt glass of the ink bottle went into full splendor.

I watched the tracing of the gold upon the inkwell and suddenly it came to me that I had been watching it for a long while, lying on my side motionless, intent on something tremendous in its scope, something that had to do with eternity and the remote lagoons that border the human soul. The moon in the persistence of its un- wavering light kept my mind still, holding it steady while it went deep—the moon that shone at the same moment through the windows of half the houses of the world and yet made each man feel that it shone alone for him, to illumine his knowledge of everlasting sad- ness.

But I should not be sad, I thought. Tomorrow will be the happiest day of my life. All the story books say so. Everyone knows that the wedding day is happy beyond compare. I must have been dreaming.

I sat up and the moonlight flattened the surface of the counterpane, released from the hump my feet had made beneath it. I swung about, letting my legs drop over the side of the bed, and reached for my wrapper. I'd decided to put my head out of the window to bring me all awake.

Leaning on the window sill, I looked across the mead- ows at the black oblongs of shadow in the corners of the stone wall on the hilltop; at the bare bent elbow of the tulip tree half way up the hill; at the blunt squared end of the rowboat's stern bumped against the farther shore of the small pond; and nearer, just below the window, at the empty circular bed in the center of the garden growing the full moon's light instead of petunias.

A cry formed itself inside my throat, pulling to be released. I kept the cry noiseless, did not allow it to come out into the open, but the force of it made my throat ache: the force born of nostalgia for the past, of my love for the scene before me, this familiar corner of my mother's country refuge—mine, also, whenever I chose to be here—of the terrible sadness I had in knowing that this night was the end of my beholding it, the end of the life of searching that was a part of it.

Oh, why had I said I would go? Why had I ever allowed the world to begin holding hands to make the circle that had closed me round? I remembered the feel of my body long ago when I was a violent little girl caught a prisoner in the arms of the opposite team playing prisoners' base in Gramercy Park; remembered the wild struggle, fighting to make myself free of the iron ring that held me. If only I might use my body that way now, wriggle and hit passionately with my fists and break through.

I let my head fall to lie in the crook of my arm on the sill while the cold air breathed along the back of my neck and the moonlight pressed on the gold of my hair as it had pressed on the gold of the ink bottle.

Presently I raised my head, and fixing my eyes directly on the moon, to clear my thoughts as a cold bath clears them, I told myself that I must return to earth once and for all so as to realize my happiness. Tomorrow I was going to be married and my husband would take me away to live with him forever and ever till death did us part—a kind, strong husband whom I could trust until the coming of Doomsday, a man who would watch over me tenderly and keep me safe. I knew this when we were together, my head on his shoulder, his arm holding me close. I shut my eyes now to regain that sensation, and the singsong words I had chanted in time to the revolving wheels of the Boston express train, bringing me home from our first meeting, came into my mind again, along with the sensation of his proximity when there in the city of his origin he had begun to show me his love: "He will guard me forever, will guard me forever."

This was the true promise of marriage for a woman: loving care, shelter from harm, the banishing of fears: fear of solitude, of death unattended. The nightmares of childhood would be washed clean from the slate of my life. This was the thing to remember, to hold.

A reassuring emanation of strength and reliability had been apparent, I remembered, during my first meeting with John Saltonstall, which had taken place at the house of my sister and her husband at Beverly Farms on the Massachusetts North Shore. I had returned only a week or so before from the gardening trip to England and France with Mrs. Cameron, and the handsome man of commanding posture there at the Sunday lunch table, in his English clothes, invited especially for me, seemed perfectly to fit that world I had left behind, a world holding power and high promise.

When lunch had ended, he asked me to go with him for a drive along the North Shore. This was in late September when the leaves were showing their splendor on a day of gleaming quiet. We set out in his Fiat sport car with victoria hood, the chauffeur wrapping a rug about my knees and climbing then, as the car began to roll, into the rumble seat at the rear. Presently we dropped the man off and continued on by ourselves for an hour or two, driving in a kind of dream wherein the sense of a fair future haunted us both, even though, at the time, we did not speak of far things. Later, I often thought of the promontory in Marblehead where we had gone that I might have a view of the widespread waters and where a speck of dust blew into my eye. How reassuring it was to feel the competence and care with which my handsome beau—for already the word had begun to apply to him—took from his pocket an impeccable handkerchief and, twisting a corner of it, removed the intruding speck. This seemed immensely more than an ordinary act of courtesy. It served as a happy augury for coming intimacies. On the days that followed, during my visit to Marjory, days of sudden frost, this new-found friend, a Galahad he had become, continued to take charge of me, sending daily presents which the chauffeur left at our door: port wine, a Jaeger blanket, and other deterrents to the cold. He himself came each day to call, and by the time my visit had ended we already knew each other well, as well as two people can know each other, I told myself now, who have walked all their lives in paths that did not meet.

The rest had moved with the celerity of light: the swift courtship in the Bedford house preceded by a mammoth box of American Beauty roses for me, their stems almost as tall as I, and a great basket of fruit and sweets from Charles & Co. for Mamma. We became engaged a month after our first meeting, and now, following two months more, we were to be married. It was all as he had wanted

it, demanded it, my husband-to-be. I too had wanted it
so, continued to want it except at the moments that crept
in unasked to wrap uncertainty, even fear, about all the
rest.

I turned from the window toward my room. My eyes
fell on three small squares of gilt standing on a shelf
above my desk. I swallowed hard. How I loved those
small gold-framed pictures which for so long had followed me about: the water color of the child on the
beach with her cherry satin slipper in her hand; the
silhouette, sharply outlined, of an eager girl looking far
into the future; the tender painting of two roses, faded
but still visible, within the embrace of their stiffly set
leaves. I would take them into the unfamiliar, widespread places where I was having to go; they would
fence in my mind, keep it in the memory of this little
room with its white plaster walls and its pumpkin-
colored floor and the green-striped curtains at the case-
ments; they would comfort me when I found myself a
stranger in strange lands.

I folded my arms close across my breast. I was cold.
The old flannel wrapper had shrunk and no longer kept
me warm. It still had its yellow color, though, a true
friend. It had been made by Mme. Blanshard four or five
years ago. Mme. Blanshard would be coming next
spring, as always, with small Juliette, that good child, to
stay in the house and make Mamma's summer dresses.
Mme. Blanshard had made Mamma's summer dresses
and mine every spring for a long, long time. Now she
would have only Mamma's to make. I should be buying
expensive clothes from a big dressmaker while my old
dresses and this wrapper stayed behind to hang limp in

the closet the way dead people's clothes were left to hang.

I shivered and got beneath the bedclothes with my wrapper on. I pulled my knees far up under my chin, making myself into a round ball, trying for warmth. The shivering went on, deep spasms of shaking that moved along the length of my body in even rhythm as though in eternal possession, cold so mixed with fright that it was not easy to tell one from the other. I must quiet it soon, find a way of getting to sleep so that I would not be unbearably tired tomorrow when the time came to put my wedding dress over my head.

"One, two, three, go!" I said aloud, commanding myself, and I unfolded my legs to stretch them between the icy sheets. Pressing hard against the footboard, I willed myself to think. Deliberately I thought of all the women since the world began who had been preparing to marry. They may well have felt as I did now, lying awake with a feeling of terror mingled with nostalgia yet underlined with high expectancy. I could do what the others had done instead of behaving as does a child left alone in the dark. Soon I should get the better of this trembling, break the rhythm, slow it until, gradually, it ceased altogether. I would lie motionless, then, like the Lady of Shalott floating along the limpid stream.

What was the most serene moment I had ever known? Coming out onto close-cropped meadows above tall sand dunes, as a girl at East Hampton, after a drive in a two-wheeled cart through scrub oak woods in summertime. The moment after slowing Jack, the gay old ex-theater horse with one blind eye, allowing him to nibble grass while I gazed over the blue sea and thought of Tristan and Isolde and their love for each other. How beautiful those moments had been!

My feet relaxed their pressure on the footboard. I burrowed deeper into the pillow. Tristan and Isolde—what marvelous love that was, pure, unfaltering love, an endless clinging together of a man and a woman beneath the forest trees, a cleaving that was beautiful until the last . . .

You were lovely, Isolde. . . . Were you never sad? . . . Far away in the deep, deep woods—

Something came to lie across my eyelids, something that had not been there earlier. I opened my eyes and saw a faint light, feeble, colorless, frail as a stillborn babe. It came through the casement, tingeing the curtains with strangeness, making a pallid watery extent of the pumpkin-colored floor.

"It's the beginning of today," I whispered, and closed my eyes tight to hold my thoughts within a tall forest where virgin trees sheltered a pair of lovers.

9

A BRIDE

WE LEFT the one-o'clock express, the Yankee Clipper running from New York to Boston, at the Back Bay Station. It was a rainy day and water fell in rivulets along the windowpanes of the swiftly moving train that carried me from my childhood home to the new one awaiting me on Commonwealth Avenue. Within the Pullman car in which we sat, my husband and I, bride and groom of a few weeks, the overhead lights shone brightly, a cushion was at my back, a footstool beneath my feet, recently purchased magazines in my lap. Everything had been done for my comfort and yet my spirit faltered, answering more to the drab scene without than to the brilliance within.

I thought back on our honeymoon spent at Jekyl Island in Georgia, at the club to which my husband belonged along with members and friends from New York, Philadelphia and Boston. The club was used by these men as a base for shooting and fishing, and the warmth of sea winds combined with stretches of sandy beach and dunes made it an alluring retreat, the more so as it was far removed from crowds. Jekyl Island, in fact, was a most exclusive place. At the moment of our visit in December and out of season, it had appeared to me almost too exclusive, there being but one other member present to share with us the grounds and the great building. A broad staircase leading upward to corridors of closed and empty rooms was used only by us, and the white-draped, unoccupied tables in the dining room had an almost mortuary air. Our table was close to a window looking out over tall eucalyptus trees hung with strips of gray Spanish moss, and as I sat waiting for lunch to appear, carried in by a colored man who must take forty-seven steps, by my count, to reach us from the kitchen door, I wondered whether the moss, rootless and air-borne, would outlast the tree which was its host. I hoped not. But it seemed an uneven battle.

On fair days we went out to walk along the beach or to follow paths through the woods where the odors torn from the underbrush by the sun were of a more exotic kind than those in our northern clime. Now and then we sat in the shelter of a dune and I read aloud to my husband from *The Oxford Book of English Verse* which I carried with me. But he, a busy man whose parents had died when he was still a boy, had had small experience in attending while another read, and I feared I had not managed to woo him toward a new habit. I began with Meredith's "Love in the Valley" and Browning's "Meeting at Night" and "Parting at Morning," which I had long loved. They seemed not to win him as I had been won. On another day I took a volume of Kipling from the club shelves and tried him with those poems which my father liked best. These did not serve either. They merely lulled him to sleep beneath the noon sun while the surf murmured its soothing refrain.

Far more enjoyable to my husband had been his forays onto the beach, gun over his shoulder, in search of shore birds as possible prey. He took me with him on these occasions to act as an aide, a kind of amateur beater on the pattern of those on the Scottish moors, that I might drive the birds in his direction. It became a game to ride a bicycle down the wood path while he waited at a given point in the open on the sands. After riding about a quarter of a mile, I came out on the beach below him where, obedient to his command, I turned and rode back against the wind, driving the birds before me. The number killed as a result of our connivance was not very great, and I was relieved, though I hardly liked to say so, when the charming small yellow-legged creatures had flown to some spot farther up the beach, there to rejoin their mates in the apparently innocent but life-preserving game of the search for sand fleas in and about the foam of the endless breakers.

On the station platform at Boston, as the porter helped me from the train steps, a smart new gilt-initialed dressing case in my hand, cinders floated on the surface of puddles, and the stairs as we went upward to ground level were darkened with damp and dirt. A horse-drawn cab awaited us above—a Timmins, as they were known —wide and swaying and redolent of manure mixed with mold, a smell peculiar to these Boston cabs. Peculiar to Boston also, I soon found, was the friendliness of the Timmins Irish driver, his knowledge of the Back Bay families whom he served and his obvious pleasure in serving them. Unlike the irascible driver of the Paris fiacre, who was known to berate his horse and to refuse a fare at the hour of lunch, unlike the driver of the Moscow droshky in the Russian novel, who fell a frequent victim to the impatience and anger of his passenger, the Timmins driver became a willing part of the situation surrounding his fare.

During our drive to 181 Commonwealth Avenue on that afternoon of our arrival, noticing that I had been struck with the coachman's affability, my husband told me the story of Mr. Jefferson Coolidge, once our Ambassador to France and a much-traveled man of the world. When, at the end of many years abroad, Mr. Coolidge decided on the return trip to Boston, he had had to brave a series of disenchantments, those brought by the unhappy parting from European friends and the sophisticated pleasures of European life. He had put up with the discomfort of the Atlantic crossing, the crude landscape viewed from the deck of the ship as she approached land where goats nibbled between strewings of tin cans in the wire-fenced back yards of ungainly wooden houses, and on the dock he had suffered from the noisy cries of newsboys, the rattle of baggage trucks, the plain, sparse look of the American scene. Reaching the Back Bay Station, he had been disheartened by its cavernous appearance, its aura of a passage to purgatory, and following his porter up the stairs, much as we had recently done, he had encountered the inevitable Timmins. When the bags were stowed inside the cab and all was in readiness for him to enter, the coachman touched his shabby top hat with the whip and inquired, "Dartmouth Street house, Mr. Coolidge, sir?" Disenchantment ceased on the instant. Where else in the world after so prolonged a passage of time could there have been a greeting such as this? Compensation indeed.

We reached the high stone stoop and entered the house of Miss Adele Thayer, which we were to occupy during the remaining winter months. Miss Thayer, a spinster now deceased, had lined the entrance hall with marble busts atop their pedestals. Some, it was explained to me, were portraits of departed ancestors, others were of the Roman emperors. Not easy to tell them apart. The house had been chosen for us by my husband's sister, Lucy Rantoul, who had also obligingly engaged the servants to staff it. They were on hand to greet us: an English butler, lean and correct, an English lady's maid who called me "Modom," a Swedish cook and her young assistant from Finland, a sweet-faced Irish chambermaid who soon became a friend, and her intended, the choreman-furnaceman. Quite a retinue and all mine to command, a queen entering her palace. Outwardly, I was as composed as the queen is by tradition; inwardly, I was bewildered, unsure, lacking the sense of reality past and present. I seemed to myself a negative replica of that positive being which once I had been. Was it thus that the wives of the Pilgrim Fathers felt on reaching the shores of Massachusetts Bay?

Upstairs a formal drawing room on the front faced a smaller room at the rear—a library for my particular use, my husband said it was to be. I glanced at it in some trepidation. On one side the walls were filled with books —novels of the past twenty or thirty years—while opposite hung a picture gallery: pictures of every kind, every shape, oils, water colors, photographs, in frames of all varieties from wide and ornate gilt to somber stained oak. They formed a pattern cleverly fitted to leave no spot vacant. A large marquetry desk in the window— my work desk it would become—inviting in itself though it was, faced this conglomerate collection of art, and I could not help comparing the room with our quiet book-lined library in New York, where a lovely collection of Italian majolicaware stood above the shelves, where a fire burned in winter on the hearth and curtains of Liberty silk cast their golden glow over all the rest.

"Better get the pictures down as soon as I can," I whispered to myself and turned away to be shown the bedrooms above.

The library and I became intimately connected during the weeks that followed our unpacking. It was here, on a stepladder, with the choreman giving me his aid, that I first became aware of a new fate in store for me. I had climbed the ladder myself, rather than he, partly from long habit caught from my father of doing things independently, partly because it was easier from this position to decide which pictures should be removed from the wall, which left hanging. As I reached for one, high under the cornice, I became giddy and would have fallen if the choreman had not come quickly forward to steady me.

"Perhaps we'd better put off the rest until tomorrow, Patrick," I said. "I think I don't feel very well just now."

"A good idea, Ma'am. We'll be done in a jiffy, come morning, we will indeed, Ma'am."

As the giddiness and feeling of general ill continued, I telephoned my sister-in-law who lived only two blocks away. She came at once and put me to bed.

"I'll phone Dr. Jackson," she said. "Best to have him look you over, though I'm pretty certain of what he'll say." And she smiled a benign smile.

Dr. Jackson, plump and persuasive and experienced, said the thing he had been expected to say: I had started a baby. I must stay in bed until I felt better and I should take things easily for the next few months.

"But, Doctor," I said, and my sister-in-law standing in the doorway listened, presumably, in dismay, "I don't know how to take things easily. I never have. And I must get the rest of those pictures off the walls of the library and I've been counting on taking violin lessons from Mr. Loeffler. Do I have to give that up?" Tears were not far away.

"I see no reason," the tactful man answered, "why you shouldn't continue with your violin provided you don't allow yourself to become too tired. Why not practice your scales sitting down? Wouldn't that be possible?"

"I suppose so," I said faintly, and managed a smile.

"And you know, my dear lady, it's a pretty splendid business in itself, that of bringing a child into the world, a first child to present to a fond husband."

"I suppose so," I said again, and gave him a real smile this time, as, at his words, an image of what the future held became vivid in my mind and heart.

That first winter of marriage, in remembrance, meant beyond all else dinner parties, lunch parties, tea parties, parties welcoming the bride in a hospitality that seemed heartfelt and widely embracing. I had much to learn of local manners, long-established usage, within this hierarchy which was my husband's Boston. Now and then I resisted, wishing to go my own way. Soon I gave this up, for my way did not count; the odds were too heavily stacked, had been stacked years before I was born.

There was, for instance, the evening party given by Mrs. Montgomery Sears early that first winter, in her beautiful house overlooking the Public Garden. Fritz Kreisler was to play the violin, to give a recital, and I had long been looking forward to it. It had seemed as though he would be playing especially for me. The invitation specified nine o'clock, and after an early dinner at home that evening we went upstairs to dress. On the way, I heard my husband tell the butler to order a Timmins to be at the door at a quarter before nine.

"But," I said, "it takes only five minutes to drive to Mrs. Sears' house from here and presumably the music won't begin until nine-thirty. Aren't you ordering the cab a half hour too early?"

"The invitation says nine o'clock," my husband answered. "And that means nine o'clock."

"It doesn't in New York," I murmured, thinking of the many late-comers to boxes at the Opera, of dinner guests often fifteen to twenty minutes behind the specified hour in a city where tardiness among the fashionably minded was taken casually and for granted.

"I wonder whether you can possibly be right," I said, resolved to dawdle over my dressing.

Presently, as I put the last pins into my topknot and as my maid Smithers was about to help me into my dress, a knock came at the door. Smithers returned to say the butler had announced that the cab waited below.

"I can't be down for ten minutes," I called to the man beyond the door. "Ask the cab to wait, please." And I went on with the business of making myself as attractive as possible. My dress was a lovely one of white-and-gold brocade and most becoming, I knew. It was a pleasure to put it on, to linger over the last touches. Finally, I pinned on the two gardenias presented me by my husband, gathered up my shoulder-length gloves and my wrap and walked majestically down the stairs, looking forward to the admiring compliments I was sure to receive when I reached ground level.

The compliments were not forthcoming. At the head of the last flight of stairs I saw my husband below, in overcoat and gloves, pacing the front hall, gold watch in hand. I stood still, disconcerted, alarmed.

"Why, what's the matter?" I asked and ran swiftly down.

"We shall be twelve or fourteen minutes late," he answered. "It's already seven minutes past nine."

I patted his arm, trying to soothe, and held out my wrap that he might place it about my shoulders. "I'm sure we'll be in good time," I said again, as we went down the stoop toward the waiting cab. He did not answer and I thought it a sad pity, with so much pleasure lying before us, that he should be thus easily upset, offended.

At the front door of Mrs. Sears's house on Arlington Street, no other carriages were discharging passengers. The house was lit in festive fashion but no soul entered the tightly closed front door. My heart sank and a little of my alarm returned. In silence my husband tipped the driver and we mounted the house steps. The door opened at our approach, opened onto emptiness, save for the servants in attendance upon it. A dignified white-haired maid in second place behind the butler put a finger over her lips in token of silence. From upstairs, the sound of a piano could be heard in the opening bars of the Mozart violin and piano Sonata in B Flat Major. Soon, I knew, Kreisler would enter with the answering sequences. The recital had begun. My husband had been right. A blush of contrition and shame spread along my cheeks as together we tiptoed up the stairs. Our hostess sat just within the music room. She did not rise but pointed, at our approach, to a couple of chairs standing empty outside. She too placed a finger on her lips. I blushed again, more in anger this time, anger at having to be instructed in the decorum surrounding music, anger with myself in having thus willfully, yet unintentionally, placed my husband in so unfortunate a position.

Gradually, I was soothed and restored by the sounds coming to me from beyond. They were beautiful— beauty of violin tone and delicate response from piano, beauty of phrasing and technique, beauty spread about as if from the arc of a fairy's wand. What more can man desire than this immense privilege, I asked myself, the privilege granted him by encountering the genius of a great composer as interpreted by a great artist?

Applause following the end of the sonata brought us to our feet. We shook hands, now, with Mrs. Sears, who said simply, "You were late." There was but one answer to this and I gave it with my whole heart. "I'm very sorry," I said. Then we took our places with the rest.

Another occasion of music at Mrs. Sears's house, an afternoon tea party, enabled me to hear a string quartet composed by Charles Martin Loeffler, the violinist, with whom I had been studying. A group of us sat listening to sounds difficult to comprehend, so unusual was the idiom, and after the first moments I postponed the effort of understanding and allowed my eyes to wander about the handsome, high-ceilinged gallery whose walls were hung with the fine collection of musical instruments made in other years by Mr. Sears. Flanking the gallery was the room that gave on the Public Garden, a room filled with flowers from our hostess's out-of-town greenhouse: great sheaves of lilies, vases of spring jonquils, hyacinths, freesias and, covering the green-and-gold lacquered surface of an ancient spinet, bowls afloat with camellias, pink, red, white. A kind of wonderland in color and scent that lingered in the memory. How many, how varied, how profound were the joys vouchsafed human beings, I thought, as I had thought so often before. They offset the evil moments many times over, being often renewed for the asking or for continual awareness of them. Whereas the others, the ugly, the tedious, the sorrowful, struck at one but seldom and lingered only from unconscious courting.

With the end of the Loeffler quartet I joined the company in the dining room for tea. There was much discussion of the music but the contributions of most, amateurs that we were, seemed not particularly valid. Our hostess had told us that the musicians would play again later, that she hoped we could remain to hear and, it was rumored, another quartet of Loeffler was to be given us.

We sat down once more, a handful of masculine music lovers free to appear at this hour and an imposing number of ladies attired for the afternoon in dresses of heavy silk, lace collars stiffly boned at the neck, high, wide-brimmed hats, their crowns swirled with passementerie or feathers. I stayed a little apart, sitting against the wall, attentive, this time, to the music. I hoped to be able to make up my mind, to decide for or against.

The musicians tuned their instruments, ever a moment of excitement that spoke of pleasures to come, the first violin gave the signal to begin and they launched into the intricacies of new music competently presented. I listened. A cello passage seemed familiar. I had heard it, I believed, not long ago. When could this have been? I listened more intently, trying to think. The viola repeated the cello passage, making it even more familiar. Then I knew. This was the same quartet we had been given earlier, before tea, played now once again as further aid to digestion, corporal, mental. I smiled. What a joke to perpetrate upon us! Who had instigated the idea? Our hostess? Loeffler himself? At any rate, there it was, and quite naturally the music on second hearing lost its air of strangeness, became by degrees a friendly acquaintance.

"Which do you like best, the first or the second?" inquired one innocent of another, when the musicians had gone to put away their instruments.

"The first, by all means. How about you?"

"I think I prefer the second but I'm not sure."

"And you?" The women turned to me standing close by, clapping decorously with gloved hands.

"The second," I answered in entire truthfulness.

Other small points of behavior, besides the important one of punctuality, were impressed upon me during the welcoming parties of those first years of marriage. At the dinners, for example, after making my entrance beside my husband, he in white tie and long tails, I in satin or brocade or crimson velvet trimmed with fur, wearing always the long gloves which were *de rigueur,* and my wedding present pearls, one luscious drop after another, I soon found it best not to linger in conversation with the host himself. Thus I avoided squandering such small talk as I might have in hand, reserving it for the dinner table where, as a bride, I would be placed upon his right. At table I learned to eat the oysters, invariably the opening course, even though I had looked on them with aversion ever since, as a girl, I had been informed that they were alive and aware of pain as they entered one's mouth. Halfway through the meal, with the arrival of the meat course, I dutifully dropped the conversation with my host and in mechanical exactitude turned to the gentleman on my right, applying myself to him until the dinner with its dessert of meringue *glacé* came to an end.

Later, in the drawing room, engaged over coffee with the ladies until the gentlemen finished their brandy and came to join us, I found that it was better to listen than to offer opinions of my own, especially on the subject of New York, which I regarded in a somewhat different light from theirs. To these Bostonians of long and settled habit, whose choice of hotel in my native city was traditionally the old Belmont opposite the Grand Central Station, New York was considered a topsy-turvy corner of the world, overweening, impervious to the orderly sequences of life, unaware of the finer human categories, fatiguing in its uproar and yet fascinating, with a kind of superiority based on size and variety, and not to be overlooked entirely. It was a place that offered fine plays and smart hats, and of these, out of deference to me, perhaps, we often talked while we waited for our husbands to appear. The rest of the conversation had to do with anecdotes of the local scene which were still new to me.

When the men came in at the end of the minutes of freedom allotted them, I moved, in obedience to custom, toward some chair in the room placed beside another empty one, there to sit until a gentleman should choose to honor me with his presence. We chatted, then, he and I, happily enough until, with my eye on the clock and sometimes with a warning signal from my husband across the room, I rose to bid my hosts good night. It devolved upon me, I had learned, as guest of honor to open the homeward exodus at approximately half an hour following the men's entrance. This, regardless of my own pleasure in the matter. Sometimes it was difficult to remember and adhere to this rule when the exchange between my after-dinner partner and me had got off to a good start.

The dinners and luncheons and teas were, in a sense, paid for by the making of polite afternoon calls. In the large porcelain bowl that stood on the hall table of our house, calling cards from the world without had accumulated almost to the brim: one more welcome to the bride and a potential building of friendship. For every card left on us, however, there had to be one left in return. And so, list in hand, each afternoon I went forth attired in a fine suit of lady's cloth, and ostrich-plumed hat, to sit in the right-hand corner of the Delaunay-Belleville landaulet which my husband had given me, driven by a chauffeur who got down from behind the wheel at

the successive houses to take from my extended fingers
the cards he would presently hand to the maid who answered the doorbell. There was, within this polite con-
vention, no question of direct contact with human beings, no invitation to enter, to converse, to substitute the
real for the pretended. The cards were symbols. And I
thought of Alice in Wonderland when the whole pack
of cards tumbled about her, bringing her awake.

My sister-in-law lived on the opposite side of Commonwealth Avenue, the "shady side," as it was called. During
the long mornings when my husband was at his State
Street office, after I had seen Alma the cook and with
her planned the food for the day, after the practice of
scales and bowing exercises on my fiddle was ended, I
crossed the Avenue to sit beside her in the bay window
of the front parlor where armchairs upholstered in dark
frieze were protected at back and arms by white anti-
macassars. There, as we talked, she knitted a baby blanket or tiny sweater for some young mother-to-be. Several of these items were to come eventually to me, to be
placed between smooth sheets of tissue in a satin-lined
bureau drawer standing in the upstairs hallway of my
husband's ancestral house at Beverly Cove, awaiting the
arrival of my baby during the month of September.

Our conversations as the hours passed had much to
do with the inhabitants of the Back Bay, family or
friends, those of whom my husband's sister did not ap-
prove, those to whom she was drawn, those who passed
the house, walking in the street below us. I was given
their histories, their habits, their likes, their dislikes.
Thus, still a stranger to many of them, I was well in-
doctrinated at her hands, able to stand on firm ground,

select the wheat from the chaff, avoid errors in point of view and behavior according to the local code. Often I seemed far from my base, caught somewhere between things real and feigned. "Let's pretend," we children said when we were small, when a rainy day kept us in the nursery. But as soon as the rain ceased and our make-believe came to an end under the bright new sun, we were once again our everyday selves. For me, during those first Boston years, the sun's shining brought small respite from make-believe. Not for some time, not until the war years in Washington brought me new courage, did I dare permit my individual feeling to color my thought and action among the Bostonians, many of whom later I came to admire and to love.

One older woman, as a matter of fact, had become my friend during that first winter, for the qualities she possessed of generosity, of imagination and goodness. I remembered when on a frosty morning in Miss Thayer's house the butler stood at the door of the library where I sat at the writing desk and announced her, saying that a lady awaited me in the reception room on the ground floor. I went down and found myself face to face with a woman in her sixties, perhaps, unremarkable in appearance save for the benignity which was hers. She had looked at me as though I were a child and she an affectionate teacher trying to encourage my efforts in working out a difficult sum at the blackboard.

"The important thing is to hold to first love," she urged. "Nothing else counts for as much as this. I wanted to tell you how an old lady feels about it. Hold on no matter what the adverse pressures." And her smile seemed a part of the sun that streaked the rug at our feet.

Another friend that I made during those first days was a relation by marriage, Lucy Rantoul's daughter Josephine, a niece of my husband. I was drawn to her at once, a golden-haired schoolgirl ten years younger than I. In spite of this difference in age, we managed to establish a bond that lasted. She was not present, naturally, during the morning talks I had with her mother. At first, indeed, we met but seldom, so busy and so various our lives were. But in summer on the North Shore we were together more and more often, and I came, as the years went by, to count on her early morning visits and on the fidelity of her feeling for me. It is pleasant to remember that the first call received by my first child was made by this girl who had waited many hours on the doorstep of our Beverly house until the baby's cry could be heard from above. Later, lovely as a young woman in a Gainsborough portrait, she married Henry Murray, a medical student who became my friend also, the pair of them destined to offer me with open hands, as the years went by, what the Apocrypha calls "the medicine of life."

The Irish servants, so prevalent in my new environment, I was drawn to because my New York girlhood had been ornamented by the Irish, especially the Gallagher sisters, Minnie in the front part of the house, Nora in my father's office. Sometimes in those days, passing St. Patrick's Cathedral, I had entered its doors to join the ever-present band of Irish on their knees, to smell the incense, murmur a brief prayer. And I should always remember the Christmas Eve Mass I had attended in company with the Gallaghers when I was an impressionable twelve or thirteen. Here in Boston, from a front window of our house on a recent St. Patrick's Day, I had enjoyed hearing the bands, watching the frantic waving of green flags, seeing the children held high in their fathers' arms while the kindly Irish cops kept a benign sort of order and the wild wind blowing from the east served to accelerate, rather than extinguish, the general spirit. Back Bay inhabitants seemed less delighted than I with the scene. They suffered, undoubtedly, from satiation in a town known as the largest Irish city in the world. "Why, the inhabitants of Galway feel closer to Boston than to their own Dublin!" I was told by way of explanation. I continued, however, in my friendly feeling, my heart going out to this race of superstitious, softhearted, bigoted people, to the servants who functioned in the basements of Boston's brownstones, climbing to their narrow beds at the top of the house up the dimly gaslit back stairs, often in stocking feet so as not to disturb their masters, braving the scorn of the Pilgrim Protestants in wearing on Ash Wednesday the black thumbprint pressed on their brows by their priest at early Mass.

These simple souls and their unpredictable ways I preferred to the haughty, infallible ministrations of the English servants who waited at home upon my husband and me: the butler who organized our table for dinner parties, providing rum-filled candies and Turkish delight to repose on the silver bonbonnières we possessed in quantity, who charged himself with keeping fresh the florist's ferns growing in a glass-lined container used as centerpiece, who thrust long-stemmed carnations into a Royal Worcester vase with acorns in *repoussé,* belonging to Miss Thayer, setting it down on the piano top in the drawing room. All without beauty or harmony, it seemed to me. Yet I did not interfere, for the thought of gainsaying so assured and elegant an individual disconcerted me. My maid Smithers also kept me in place with her highly professional air. At night, entering my room to help me undress, she timed the brushing of my hair, keeping it rigorously to ten minutes.

"Very good for the scalp, I'm told, Modom."

"It must be, Smithers, of course," I agreed, and I wondered each night how I could bring this custom to an end. In the morning she knelt at my feet to put on my stockings and shoes, a practice I eventually managed to stop.

My baby arrived, as Dr. Jackson had long ago predicted, at the middle of September. She was born, a sweet, fair-haired little girl, in the house at Beverly and in the bed where her father was born thirty-three years earlier. It had taken her long, long hours to decide on entering the world. No amount of walking the piazza floor, as I was ordered to do, no amount of responding, from a deep winged chair, to the pains which wildly attacked, nothing was availing during that seemingly endless night and morning and afternoon when she strove to present herself to us. Finally I was anesthetized by means of the ether which was a standby in the medical circles of Boston, where in 1830 its properties had been discovered by Dr. Morton. The ether cap was pressed over my nose and mouth by the faithful Dr. Jackson, who became quite exhausted from the effort of properly dealing with me atop the wide spaces of the immense family bed.

I too was exhausted, weary with the effort of giving

birth tied to so much else that was new, and I lay without moving for several days thereafter, glad of my husband's happiness and pride in becoming a father, glad
that I could rest, that nothing was at present asked of
me save the suckling of my babe at my breast. I lay there
listening to the waves breaking quietly on the shore beneath my window. I lay thinking of God and eternity,
of life and death, and I wondered about the future, what
it might disclose as I grew older and this babe became
a mother in her turn; gentle thoughts they were and sad,
a sadness that enveloped the whole world and all the
people who dwelt in it.

On an evening a few days after the baby's arrival we
were invited to a party where the wizard Houdini was
to perform his remarkable tricks. I could, of course, not
go, but my husband, dressed for the evening, came to
stand beside my bed before leaving, and in an effort to
rouse me from the apathy into which I had fallen he
promised to describe, when morning came, each of
Houdini's feats. This was to be a smart party given by
smart people, and as I gave myself over to darkness,
head on my pillow, I wondered why this quality came
to attach itself to certain among us rather than to others
similarly placed. Not an enviable quality, was it, one
of extreme fashion tied to power? For power in the
hands of some meant, by contrast, humiliation for others.
It smacked of the days when the noble held power of life
and death over the serf. "Arise, Sir Knight," that phrase
used upon the elevation of the commoner to a position
more lofty than the previous one, even this was tinged
with the inference of past abasement. Strange that in
England many of the poets had been willing to accept

knighthood. They did not have need of a prop of this sort, did they, with a whole world of fair images to command? Robert Browning, my mother once told me, had become a consistent diner-out in fashionable London after the death of his dear Elizabeth Barrett. What a disappointment that knowledge had brought to me who believed no more beautiful poem existed for man to dream of than Browning's "Saul." Had not the writing of this alone been sufficient to keep its author continually nourished?

The sound of the sea blended now with the sound, nearer by, of soft rain and automobile wheels spinning water on their endless rounds. Gradually solitude carried me to the far dark places whence comes its essence, and soon, drifting slowly downward, I was asleep. I dreamed, emerging from curious confusion, of a sudden sequence that portended well for humanity as I watched a line of people approach a ticket office in the distance. Cool green grass was all about them and they chatted amicably. I got into line, glad to join them. Presently I noticed that as people left the ticket office, things seemed to go less well. Here they were downcast where the others were gay. Taking my turn at last before the window, I was confronted by the Devil—horns, tail, red garb and all the rest.

"Oh," I said. "I beg your pardon. I wanted to buy a ticket to heaven."

The classic Mephistophelean laugh exploded as I spoke. "You are all after the same thing," the Devil said, "every last one of you. Don't you know, poor fools, that there's no such place as heaven?"

I woke in terror, and the darkness brought neither

assurance, comfort, nor any other form of aid. I was alone face to face with my soul, alone between the Devil and the abyss he had created for it to dwell in, an abyss rapidly assuming the shape of a boundless vacuum, a vacuum that all the ages of time could not serve to fill.

A soft knock at the door. "May we come in, the baby and I? She's been asking for her mother," the nurse said.

"Oh, come in, Miss Gray. Do, please come in," I answered. "I was feeling very lonely here by myself in the dark."

10

EXCURSIONS

As SPRING ARRIVED, after the advent of my first baby, I was invited by my husband to take a trip with him to Europe.

"Would you like to go abroad for a while this summer?" he asked me one sunny day when the trees on Commonwealth Avenue were unfurling their pale green buds.

"Oh, I'd love to go!" I said. "How wonderful!" My heart leaped with joy at the prospect of new discovery, and I felt as a child does who has been promised a doll's house or an army of tin soldiers. "Shall we be gone long?" I asked.

"About six weeks," he answered. "I have business that will keep me for a week or so in London. We can make a few visits to the English country and wind up in Scotland where old Mr. Alexander Cochrane has hired a moor. He's asked us to be there August twelfth, opening day of the grouse shooting."

"How wonderful," I said again, there being nothing

else that so well expressed my feeling, and my imagination went rioting off into places that held enchantment as a garden basket holds roses and peonies. "What about the baby?" I asked.

"We'll engage a capable trained nurse to look after her and supervise the household."

"What if she misses me and is unhappy?" My heart sank and the flowers I had conjured up began to wither.

"She'll be all right provided she has regular food and sleep. Babies of that age live from moment to moment. Their memories are short. Besides, Lucy will be delighted to come in every day to see how things are going."

We sailed in July on a Cunarder from New York. This fact added glamour to the trip, seeming to toss us at the outset into a larger world than that we might encounter had we sailed from Boston, as many travelers from the Back Bay preferred to do.

"What of all the clipper ships, the East India traders, that once set sail from Salem, an even smaller port than Boston?" my husband inquired when I told him of my feeling. "Those ships circled the globe, touched at almost any port you can mention."

"That's true," I murmured, put properly in my place. All the same, I was happy to be sailing from a pier along the Hudson River of my native town. Although I had lived away from home for almost a year and a half, I had not entirely got over an underlying need for familiar things.

On board ship were several partners of the house of J. P. Morgan. We sat with them at table in the dining saloon and they shared with us the pounds of fine coffee

and the barrel of oysters with which Mr. Morgan indulged his friends. Very gay it was for me, the only lady
at table with four or five gentlemen.

In London we stayed at the Hotel Stafford in St.
James's Place opposite the narrow entry into the Green
Park. A most romantic spot this park was then to me
because of the setting of the novels of Thackeray and
others, because the house where Samuel Rogers had
given his famous breakfasts for poets and writers was
also here. I had often in the past said to myself that a
pleasant place in which to spend my declining years
would be one overlooking the Green Park.

I had been in London last with Mrs. Cameron and
Elizabeth Hoyt, remaining there for a time in lodgings
on Sloane Square before we set out to make visits to
Mrs. Cameron's friends in the country. The London stay
had coincided at that moment with the death of King
Edward VII, and we watched his magnificent funeral
cortège during several hours from the parapet belonging
to Mrs. Potter Palmer on Carlton House Terrace. We
had stood, Elizabeth and I, leaning our elbows on the
stone railing of the parapet, hanging far out the better
to see the Coldstream Guards and the Grenadiers and
the fine dignity of the Scottish Pipers, their kilts swinging in a rhythm that matched the slow pace of their step,
the mournful and moving lament of their eerie song.

Now I was in London as a married woman and the
mother of a child. I shared my pleasure with a husband
on an equal basis, no longer restricted by the decorum
suitable to a *jeune fille*. Already I had been taken on
several unusual expeditions, one of them to the shop at
the foot of St. James's Street belonging to Berry Brothers,

purveyors of wines and liquors to His Majesty the King, there to sample the sherries and the port wine which my husband planned to have sent us in Boston. Arriving at the shop, we had been received with immense courtesy by one of the Messrs. Berry, who sat behind an old-fashioned, roll-top desk near the door and who rose to greet us, his incoming guests. We were then placed, one after the other, in balancing chair scales that dated from the era of William and Mary, and our weights were carefully recorded in a massive leatherbound book. The wine tasting, which presently began, was conducted in meticulous fashion with especial emphasis brought to the sherry which later would be shipped to us in wood, and by the time I had finished sampling the delicious amber liquid, sipping it from one glass after another, I was quite tipsy and glad to be released from the vaults and guided into the open air.

The Malmaison carnations of London were my particular delight. They were favorites, I was told, of Mr. Morgan, whose gardener grew them in quantity under glass there in England. Impossible, apparently, to reproduce at home these lovely cousins to our garden pinks with their wide spread, their purple and crimson colors, their delicious concentrated odor. My husband indulged me in my passion for these exotic blooms, often presenting me with one to pin to the lapel of my jacket, and of other flowers our sitting room, with its chintz-covered furniture, was always full. Pleasant it was also to be a part of that man's world for which London so well provides, to see in shop windows the gloves, scarves, ties, waistcoats, the bright-hued suspenders, cuff links, shirt studs, appurtenances of a polite and traditional society, a society which my husband seemed to fit as though reared in it from boyhood onward.

We went often to the theater in London, to the magical English playhouses. The climax of our entertainment came on an evening spent watching the Russian Ballet of Diaghilev. Here, seated in comfortable stalls, surrounded by a sophisticated and discriminating audience in evening dress, we saw the beautiful and greatly loved Karsavina, of enviable prestige, dance the role of the Fire Bird to the music of Stravinsky. From my seat close below the stage I dwelt on every motion made by the lovely creature, I admired her grace, was touched by the poignant quality of her gesture, smiled at her swift flashes of humor. My admiration, my adoration, reached such heights that I was reminded of the time years back when, as a girl, I fell in love with Ethel Barrymore watching her play the part of Madame Trentoni in *Captain Jinks of the Horse Marines.* In bed that night the long familiar emotion of hero worship held me delightfully awake, as of old, through the hours when most men slumber. How truly wonderful were the stirrings of the heart in response to beauty, I whispered to myself, falling at last into sleep.

I could not then foresee that ten or twelve years later I should again be brushed by the spirit of the beautiful Karsavina when, at the behest of an American writer friend in Paris, I visited the studio of Madame Gontcharova, the painter and designer of scenery for the Russian Ballet. "She lives precariously," my friend said, "according to our standards at any rate. An unorganized, courageous sort of existence. She seems to have little understanding of money. You might perhaps want to help by buying one of her pictures."

We climbed four flights to the top floor of a rundown house on the rue de Seine, a street leading to the clock tower of the Chamber of Deputies and the Luxembourg Garden. It was a picturesque part of Paris, and Madame Gontcharova's studio was in keeping with it. I might have been entering the quarters of Rodolfo in *La Bohème*. The door was opened by a woman of no particular age. Her chestnut-colored hair was brushed back and pinned merely for convenience, her dress was of worn black and she herself unremarkable but for her eyes which held one by the expression they had of endurance and compassion. They brightened on seeing us, and she led the way into a room filled with human beings, several of them seated about a center table. Others stood before the mantelpiece, and I noticed an incongruous gathering of objects upon the shelf behind them: a plate holding slices of cake, battered tubes of oil paint, a pincushion stuck with crescent brooch, pins and needles, and a hairbrush. Near the window stood an artist's easel, vacant save for a ballet slipper of faded blue satin hanging by a ribbon from one corner.

Madame Gontcharova guided us to the table which I had seen on entering, and she placed us opposite a young woman with an extraordinarily white skin, enormous eyes, black hair parted in the middle, sleek and smooth, and drawn low into her neck. A ballet dancer, I decided, and smiled as she offered me a cup of tea from the copper samovar before her.

"We celebrate our Russian Easter during this period," our hostess said. "I am so glad you are come just now, for you will be able to eat our Russian cake, the kind made for these holy days."

Our entertainment continued as the minute hand of
my watch traveled well beyond the half hour and there
was no mention as to the object of our visit although my
friend had told Madame Gontcharova that I was interested in her work. The hope of making a sale seemed
at the moment beside the point, and I felt myself a part
of a Turgenev novel wherein the company assembled
about a samovar loses all sense of time while conversation takes its ardent but desultory way through the
progression of the hours.

I rose at last and moved toward the empty easel. "May
I see some of your pictures, Madame Gontcharova?" I
asked.

"You are sure your appetite is satisfied? This comes
first." She lingered at the table. "One more cup of tea?"

"No, thank you," I answered, and touched the hanging ballet slipper with my finger.

"Ah, this is the slipper of Karsavina, our great dancer.
You have seen her, perhaps?"

"Yes, I have. I saw her dance the Fire Bird when
Diaghilev brought the ballet to London several years
ago."

"She is very beautiful, yes?"

"She is the most beautiful person I've ever seen."

The others gathered about us as we talked, and my
young friend of the samovar seemed particularly interested.

Madame Gontcharova explained, "Karsavina is our
heroine, a kind of goddess she has become, married now
to an English diplomat and no longer to be seen dancing."

"What a pity!"

"A pity, yes, for us. But not so for her, perhaps. She is much loved and guarded. This other life of the artist can be *très dure*. She will not now be obliged to grow old upon the stage. So we keep here the slipper in which she danced *Le Spectre de la Rose*. It is a remembrance."

My heart went out to these touching friends of the lovely Karsavina and I wished them well, wished that their lives, as time passed, should not become *très dure*. Presently I bade them good-by, carrying away two Gontcharova paintings, one an oil, the other a water color done in the semi-abstract manner of the period, yet as Russian in essence as the Easter cake and the samovar.

In response to an invitation from Nancy Astor, long-time friend of my husband, we went out to spend a weekend at Cliveden, the Astor country seat on the Thames. Another guest in the house was William Borden, Prime Minister of Canada. Our hostess, at that time, was much engaged in politics. Although she had not yet obtained her seat in the House of Commons, the welfare of her adopted land was of real importance to her. Mr. Borden's presence in England, then, had something to do, we were told, with the partial promise that Canada might build a battleship or two to add to the strength of the Royal Navy. And Nancy Astor's weekend job was to fix the tentative promise into permanence. Whether or not this was the underlying object, she enchanted the middle-aged Minister by her wit and her logic and her charm. We, her guests, sat at table in the dining room, holding to silence for long minutes between courses, while the servants waited without, entering the room only when summoned by their mistress' bell, and we listened avidly to her talk which went all the way from the affairs of the world and of the state to tales of the Virginia hills and the Negroes who had surrounded her when she was a girl.

My own chief interest of that weekend, aside from the beauty of the house and the grounds, flowing terraced and green to the river, was my visits to the nursery where three or four of the Astor children were in the capable hands of an English nanny and a young assistant nursemaid. Each afternoon, following a prolonged tea-drinking in the great hall, my hostess summoned me to follow her along the two upward flights until, arrived at the section of the house given to youth, we entered a large, pleasant room having a life as full, as well equipped, as secure, as the one we had left below. Pink-cheeked children and their attendants in broadly bibbed aprons were in full and equable possession of this corner of the world, while before the hearth fire, necessary in the damp of the English climate even during the summer, the white-haired nanny sat undressing the baby in her lap. On a clothes horse near the fire small garments were in process of drying, and the steam they emitted brought a gentle nostalgia for my childhood, the flannels of snowy winters spread before the coal fire in my early-morning bedroom. My own babe, awaiting me at home, I reflected, would be warming her toes in the sunshine of an August afternoon.

From England and summer warmth we went north into the enfolding mists of Scotland, to Pitlochry in Perthshire and the house named "Cromlix" with its rolling moorlands, engaged by Mr. Cochrane for the benefit of his children, his grandchildren and their friends. All was astir, when we arrived, with the prospect of the opening season on the twelfth of August, for the shooting of grouse. This was essentially a man's pastime and the required equipment was being readied: guns oiled, cartridge boxes filled, clothing assembled, the tweed knickerbockers and caps and waterproof shoes with their leather thongs essential on heather-grown moors. Among those in authority, plans were made for the organization of the shoot in the eight or ten butts which tomorrow would confront the beaters of the birds. These butts were being delegated each to one among "the guns." The best shots were assigned the center butts where the flight of the birds would be heaviest, those less experienced were placed at the ends where fewer birds would appear and where, also, shots of bad aim could do least harm to neighbors.

My husband was an excellent shot and he was given one of the best butts. As a favor seldom granted, I was permitted to accompany him on the opening day and I stood beside him, my interest vivid and sustained, waiting for the birds to appear. Everything about us was still, everyone in suspense, guns primed, until with a sound of whirring wings and the shouts of the beaters who with long sticks drove the birds on, these were suddenly, wildly over our heads, a flock of feathers streaking toward safety. The flight was answered by a rapid fusillade which continued as the guns swung about to face the rear until, at last, the grouse that had managed to escape were gone beyond reach. Then began the tally of birds bagged, the beaters gathering up the dead and wounded strewn over the ground before and behind.

This performance, often repeated, accelerated the beat of my heart and brought pride in my husband's prowess. It brought also, so contradictory are the emotions of human beings, a sadness for the wanton annihilation of these many birds, helpless in the face of man's schemes. I recognized such a feeling as one more instance of feminine weakness, but I could not drive it away as the beaters drove the birds. Earlier, at the outset of our marriage, my husband had hoped to make a shot of me in my own right, but even though I learned, after practice, to hit a glass bottle swinging from the limb of a tree, I had continually failed to pull the gun trigger upon a live bird.

After that first morning at Cromlix I did not return to the butts and instead stayed at home to read and work on my fiddle, going before lunch for a walk across the moors through miles of ankle-high heather noisily scraping my shoes. I moved into the permeating damp of a Scotch mist that left fairy cobwebs on bushes and a fringe of moisture along my eyelashes and brought an ephemeral beauty to the molded contours of valleys and the lovely colors of hillsides. One morning I came on a painter at his easel, out to gather onto his canvas the purples and greens of the surrounding background. He was Howard Cushing, husband of one of Mr. Cochrane's daughters, and his quiet smile served to offset the frown of application on his forehead.

"Out for a walk?"

"Yes, it's so delicious, this damp country."

"I agree. Wonderful to paint."

"The mist doesn't get in your way?"

"Not a bit. Better than continuous sunshine."

"It is, isn't it? Suits the lay of the land and somehow it's not in the least melancholy or depressing."

"No one with you?"

"The others are waiting for the sun."

"They can get that in the Boston suburbs." He looked down onto his canvas and took up a brush. I moved away.

Each day at lunchtime donkeys laden with baskets slung over the saddle ambled into a hollow below the butts. Behind them came servants carrying the various parts of a trestle table, linen, etc. Soon the table was set up as though in a dining room, and a hot lunch accompanied by small goblets of sherry was served us, recurrent manna. At evening I was now and then summoned to take part in the entertainment of the house party by playing my violin. One of the guests was a good accompanist and I enjoyed our moments of music together, the meditative quality of the large living room where we gathered, the shaded lights, the immense open fire, the silence of people who had been in the open during much of the day.

Difficult to bring pleasures such as this to an end, to leave Cromlix and its surrounding opulence of moor and sky at the end of two weeks. Time was up, however, our ship soon to return to New York. Awaiting us at home were family and friends, and the affairs of my husband to be resumed. More important, there was my babe to recapture with her quick smile that answered mine, her small yielding body to hold in my arms. The line broken by our voyage was thus to be spliced again into familiar continuity, the laws of orderly, everyday existence to be enforced once more.

Following the first war, several years later, I was taken from home to accompany my husband on a journey even farther afield. We had been invited to visit a Harvard classmate of his, Peter Augustus Jay, our Ambassador to Romania. With the meticulous care governing our moves, plans for the trip were made well in advance, hotel accommodations engaged, railroad tickets secured and all other details requiring supervision smoothed so they should not rise up to bother us. How entirely pleasant and easy it all was and how I loved to be thus cosseted and spoiled. "Better see to it that you deserve all these fine things," a voice of warning now and then whispered, a voice to which I paid not too much heed, taking fair fortune very much for granted in the way that mankind has.

We landed at Cherbourg from one of the large liners and took the boat train to Paris. This initial train journey into France brings ever-renewed pleasure to the traveler, with the intimate view it gives of the countryside, neat little gardens where vegetables grow beneath inverted glass bells, two-wheeled jogging farm carts painted blue, school children in black aprons, leather belts drawn tight about their slim waists, churches gray with age, spires pointing toward the cloud-embroidered sky. I sat in the continental carriage, leaning against the well-padded, lace-covered back, watching the scene while the agile train sped like some headlong chariot of old, and I listened with amusement—telling myself how fortunate I was to be thus flung into the scenes I had known since childhood—when the engine let go its shrill high shriek, a signal at grade crossings attended by saluting guards in uniform.

In Paris we stayed at the Ritz in a room that gave onto the quiet of an inner garden, and our breakfast we ate between French windows opened wide to let in the scent of lilacs brought by the Paris spring. Out in the street surrounding the Place Vendôme were all the enticements a woman could find in the way of alluring adornment: the famous houses for the designing and making of dresses, the jewelers, perfumers, vendors of artificial flowers that miraculously reproduced the real. Delightful it was to stand below Napoleon's column that went loftily upward and to know oneself a part of this wealth so abundantly proffered.

I went one morning to the Maison Chéruit to order an evening dress suitable for the diplomatic world into which we were about to penetrate.

"What sort of evening dress does Madame desire?" the knowing *vendeuse* inquired.

"Not a ball dress, yet appropriate for a large, formal dinner," I explained.

"I have Madame's idea. Just leave it to me to carry out. Will Madame return, perhaps, in two days for her first fitting?"

The dress was perfect, made of silver lamé in the style of a peplos worn by a Greek Aphrodite, and it was most becoming, my husband said. With this addition to my wardrobe and a traveling suit from the competent tailor Creed, I felt equipped for the journey ahead, a journey taking us all the way to Constantinople by means of the Orient Express, that romantic train so much written of in novels and plays, the spine giving off those skeletal bones that spread their lines of transportation across Europe. Day by day we sped on through countries which previously had been for me but divisions of a map to be studied, and at night our sleep was interrupted by the flashing of lights in our stateroom as we crossed some new frontier where passports were to be examined.

At Constantinople, St. Sophia seemed a most beautiful basilica, with its air of opulent tradition, and the Byzantine remains spread over the city brought a kind of wonder to the onlooker and awe and sorrow also because of the power of long-forgotten dreams manifest in them and because of the unsparing dissolution of magnificence wrought by time. The famous bazaar held us for hours as we moved a little at a time from one underground booth to another, evading, with a technique that grew rapidly in skill, the importunities of vendors who urged their wares in most positive fashion. Here my husband presented me with a pair of rococo stickpins, large and topheavy with cabochon emeralds and baroque pearls, examples of the jewels once in everyday use by the Russian nobility. Indeed, the bazaar held many souvenirs from old Russia: monogrammed cigarette boxes of silver or shell, ladies' gold-encrusted card cases, brooches, bracelets, earrings, the splendid ornaments of an aristocracy in flight, discarded of necessity as barter for funds that would carry their owners away from the mortal danger attendant upon revolution. I wore my stickpins on either side of a dress cut with a square neck, but the enjoyment I had in them was tempered by the thought of their rightful owner bereft now of fortune and fair winds, bereft perhaps of family and friends in some country far from home.

Our visit to the Jays began at the port of Constantsa on the Black Sea. It had been arranged in advance that we should embark from Constantinople on a small coastwise ship which would set us down the day following. Peter Jay had offered to meet us at the port and escort us by train to Bucharest. The steamer, as it chugged through the crowded, hit-or-miss traffic of the Bosphorous and on into the tranquillity of the Black Sea, seemed a part of a theater scene. It had the cardboard cutout quality possessed by the simulated ship drawn by a swan that carried Lohengrin ashore.

We arrived in due course and were met on the dock by our host, who had our baggage transferred to the waiting train—one, we presently learned, chartered especially for us, there being no regular train scheduled to synchronize with the coming of our ship into port. A new sort of splendor this was, difficult to apprehend, for I had never expected to share a privilege peculiar to royalty, high-placed financiers, traveling circuses and Presidential candidates. The casual talk between the two men, however, as the train sped—talk of Harvard and mutual classmates, of politics at home, of the careers and future intentions of the two—brought to the trip a cast of the everyday more tolerable than that of grandeur and high authority.

The American Embassy at Bucharest, with its garden and unconventional interior, was a pleasant place in which to be received, and Mrs. Jay made us feel instantly at home until we were told that King Carol and Queen Helen and their retinue were coming to dine that evening. The grand world was once again in prospect, stirring the imagination so that I could give only a small residue of my attention to our sightseeing tour of the city on that afternoon. We returned to find the Jays and their secretaries engrossed in the business of seating arrangements based on the rites of protocol in which a single small blunder might bring on the repercussions of disaster. My husband and I were, naturally, of no use in this highly specialized world, and we remained away in our rooms, as befitted ordinary people, to await the hour of preparation for the party.

The party, though absorbing in the opportunity it gave us to observe a scene unfamiliar to us, was not actually gay. Gaiety, I came then to understand, could not attach itself to a formal dinner graced by royalty. Impossible for Their Majesties to permit a letting down of the bars onto those free spaces where spontaneity holds sway.

At the end of dinner we women entered the drawing room where the Queen, surrounded by her ladies, went to sit in a far corner. Meanwhile the King remained for long minutes with the gentlemen in the smoking room. It had been explained to my husband and me that we were not to address the King or Queen unless to answer a question put to us. So I attached myself to a group of guests apart from the royal party. Presently Mrs. Jay, accompanied by one of the ladies in waiting, stood before me. I rose to my feet.

"Her Majesty wishes to have a little chat with you," I was told.

My heart set up a great pounding as I walked across the room, making my curtsy before seating myself at the Queen's side. The conversation was at first of the usual pattern between strangers, having to do with my place of origin, the number of my children, the profession of my husband, and so forth. Then, in a tone that came suddenly alive, Her Majesty asked, "Where was this dress made that you are wearing? In Paris, I daresay. It is a very pretty one."

"Thank you," I answered, instinctively pressing between my fingers one of the pleats in the silver lamé. "It *is* pretty, I think. Yes, it came from the Maison Chéruit."

"Very pretty indeed," she repeated.

"You see, they knew—I told them there—that we were coming to Bucharest, possibly to meet the King and Queen. And so they did their best."

Her Majesty smiled. But now the conversation flagged, and before long I gave my place to the lady in waiting who hovered nearby. Later, when the party ended, we were told it had been an entire success measured, presumably, by standards not available to us.

During the morning that followed, word came from the palace that the Ambassador and Mrs. Jay and their guests were invited to lunch with the King and Queen: a royal edict of sorts. On arrival, we were shown into a small living room, obviously a spot which the family occupied at intimate moments: deep sofas, tables strewn with magazines, a piano adorned with leather-framed photographs, the earmarks of home. We were the only lunch guests and Their Majesties wore country tweeds. In the dining room Mrs. Jay sat on the King's right while I was placed on his left. We took turns answering his questions, trying to think of items of interest that might hold his attention. This was not easy. He was dull and unresponsive in a stubborn, even cruel, sort of way, and there seemed no means of bringing light and kindness to his face. His Queen, on the other hand, though poised within the dignity of her role, possessed a gentle graciousness which was illumined by a vivacity that, I could see, charmed the men on either side of her.

Our entertainment, following lunch, was of the sort that the young and unoccupied resort to on a rainy day. While the King talked to Peter Jay and to my husband of his hunting exploits, the Queen got out her photograph albums and showed us snapshots of the family and their entourage: at the sea in bathing costume, on horseback, in groups beside garden beds staring into the sun.

"Here is my son, Michael, and his little friends," she said with a smile presently, pausing before she turned the page. "He was then eight years old and this was his birthday party." The boy, I could see, was his mother's solace in a difficult world. I hoped he might always treat her well.

Before we took our leave, Queen Helen presented my husband with a cabinet photograph of herself which she signed with affability. She had lost her heart to him, obviously—a thing entirely understandable to me, with his fine looks, his upright and dignified bearing. "Poor woman," I murmured to myself, "think what, by contrast, she must put up with."

On departing, my husband and I did our best to emulate the ease with which the Jays made their bows of farewell and went from the room, according to etiquette, facing Their Majesties, backs to the door. We were more clumsy and for me there was a further difficulty for I felt the whole paraphernalia attending regal ceremony to be rather absurd. How fortunate I was, I thought presently, making my dignified way down the stairs of the palace, to be placed within spheres free of hierarchies, recurring formalities, to be able to run over the meadows with my children on a spring day, go barefoot along the sands, laugh at sudden joy. How much, how very much, I had to be thankful for.

The return journey brought us overnight to Budapest, where, at noon on the day that followed, we were given a luncheon at the Hotel Luna Palota by the secretaries of the British Legation, one or two of whom we had already known. They engaged a *Tzigane* orchestra for our entertainment and we listened eagerly to the wild music that stirred us with the passionate rhythm which is a part of the Gypsy nature. Later we were taken to climb the hills overlooking the old town. Delicious it was to walk after so many hours in trains and motors, to labor up steep paths, wind through great dark woods, stumble downward, on and on, slipping, sliding, laughing.

On board the Orient Express once again, headed for Paris, headed for home, I suffered for my extravagance with muscles so stiff as to keep me almost motionless during several days. We are doubtless not intended to be continually pelted with the flowers that grow, pluck and hold them for our own, unless in some degree we pay for the pleasure they bring, I said to myself, and turned my head, as the train raced along, to look out upon meadows where peasants cultivated the grain beneath the sun of early summer.

II

LIFE AND DREAMS

WHEN I was a young lady reaching twenty, several years before my marriage, there were dreams that hovered about me clinging, persistent, throwing me off balance with new delight, coloring episodes in their onset and flight, dreams so clear and bright that, although I believed them eventually buried, they were to have a serious impact on my future. There were also humorous episodes that arose, gay, absurd, momentarily upsetting my dignity, dissolving it as a patiently built fort of sand is dissolved by the unwatchful tide. Sorrow I had not yet met in the full force of its sinister power. It appeared to have no lasting part in my life, little desire to strike at me deeply. It was reserved, I believed, for the weak and unfortunate, those whose vitality lacked zest, and I could not help believing myself rather apart from these fainthearted beings.

One of the dreams coloring my thought at that time was born in Boston where I had briefly gone at the invitation of a Harvard senior to see the annual play and attend the dance given by the Hasty Pudding Club. There, from the windows of a house on Commonwealth Avenue, I had on a weekday morning watched the gentlemen of the Back Bay walk to their offices on State Street. They walked beneath the elms that stood above the central path, leading northward to the Public Garden, and their aspect compelled me. For they moved not as the ordinary creature does who hustles or loiters on his undistinguished way. These men wore an air of composure, along with their carefully cut clothes—an air of circumspection subtle in the things it implied of high destiny, of precedent long established. Heroes they might have been from a Meredith novel or from one by Henry James, heroes they became for me. How fine, I whispered to myself, to join this band of the chosen, to become the wife of one of these splendid beings. An enviable existence hers would be. For a long moment on that sunny morning I allowed myself to dwell upon this dream.

At the Arlington Street end of the Avenue, giving upon the gardens, there stands a statue of Alexander Hamilton designed by the sculptor William Rimmer, graceful in its dignity, spare, decisive, with robe gracefully flowing. This statue I saw for the first time on the Sunday morning that followed the Hasty Pudding dance as I returned from a drive with my young student friend in a horse-drawn buggy. The buggy had been hired from a livery stable, and the horse, though lacking in the finer points of conformation, was sturdy and tractable. We had driven out to Brookline along the borders of Jamaica Pond and were returning at the hour when the Sunday church services were ending. We drove in happy mood on a day of permeating sunshine, well satisfied with our adventure and restored in vigor after the fatigues of the previous evening. We felt entirely superior to the promenading disciplinarians of the city streets who appeared earth-bound as we outstripped them in our winged chariot while my companion uttered humorous comments which I found irresistible.

"What's the joke?" a boy shouted when for a moment we paused at a crossing. I could not have answered. I did not know what the joke was. I knew only that I was young in a young world which looked upon me with apparent favor.

We passed Berkeley Street on our homeward way, approaching the Rimmer statue, and my companion touched the horse's back with the whip. The animal lunged awkwardly, no longer amenable, and as though in answer to our renewed laughter, jerked himself free of the wagon shafts to move in lone purpose along the Avenue. My friend leaped over the dashboard, reins in hand, following the horse on foot, and I was left sitting alone in the buggy while the congregation from Emmanuel Church around the corner came to a halt in order to stare.

Later, after my marriage, when I moved to Commonwealth Avenue to stay, the statue of Hamilton and the horseless buggy remained confounded in my memory while the gentlemen of the Back Bay, my husband among them, continued to be wrapped in romance and the dream. Reality then, for me, was the life of music, which, momentarily interrupted by the advent of a new baby, continued nonetheless as of old, merely transferred from New York and Paris to Boston. Natural and right, it seemed, to concentrate on violin practice and the lessons given me first by Charles Loeffler, a local god, later by Felix Winternitz who headed his department at the Conservatory of Music.

An added source of solid pleasure were the weekly concerts of the Boston Symphony Orchestra. As a regular subscriber to the Friday afternoon performances, I sat in the first balcony close above the stage and I came to know by sight the various musicians: the concertmaster, who took his place at the first violin desk with a trifle more authority of manner than the others; the first cellist, bending low over his fingerboard during sostenuto passages that moved as a song of love; the full-blown, ruddy cheeks of the bassoon player negotiating difficult *vivace* runs inserted by some unwary composer into the score in defiance of the ponderous character of the instrument. There was the lady harpist with graceful fingers and flowing sleeves who contributed to the performance after long moments of withdrawal when she sat beside the towering harp, grown cold, hands in her lap like some well-behaved schoolgirl. How was she able to be so certain of her timing, I wondered, how count so accurately the bars of music she must travel in silence? The chief drummer was a major force at his task of rampageous co-operation with other instruments, his eager, explosive entry onto the scene, the wild speed of his manipulation and, during a pause, the affecting way in which he bent low to place an ear against the drum, tapping it interrogatively as the orchestra played on, making sure that recent attacks had not forced it out of tune.

The orchestra conductor was ever compelling in his role of taskmaster and purveyor of inspiration, in his display of technique, power, idiosyncrasy. When first I became regular in my attendance at the concerts, Dr. Karl Muck, recently arrived from Berlin, was in charge. His reputation in Germany, in all of Europe, was supreme, and the orchestra trustees in Boston felt themselves fortunate in persuading him across the seas. Then came the First World War and the necessity for rounding up those German sympathizers who might, conceivably, cripple the Allied cause. Dr. Muck became suspect, and as he rehearsed his men for the Holy Week presentation of Bach's splendid *St. Matthew Passion,* he was taken into custody by the police. To artists and musicians, the sensitive and perhaps impractical among human beings, this was a gross act of malfeasance, the more so as he was for some time held in one of the precinct stations along with the drunken and the wayward. At this grave moment, Mrs. Gardner drove from her palace at Fenway Court to call on him, bringing him delicacies and small luxuries by way of assuagement.

"Mrs. Jack Gardner feeds Karl Muck through prison bars!" the newspaper headlines screamed.

It was during Dr. Muck's tenure, in the first year I occupied my balcony seat, that I clung to a romantic dream having to do with a fellow member of the audience. She sat, a woman of striking personality, a few rows below me, and the back of her blond head, heavy hair brushed smoothly upward, was visible to me whenever I chose to look. I looked often because of the pleasure I had in her gracefully upright posture and because her enjoyment of the music appeared to be one with mine. A bond formed itself between us—at least it seemed to me a bond, although we had not met, not spoken—and she became for me a kind of goddess of music, a Saint Cecilia. On the day we were introduced by a mutual friend, I found that in confronting reality my dream need not be shattered. The name of the goddess was Mrs. Frederick Lowell and I was destined in future to be often with her and her family, making music with them, playing Mozart, Haydn, Beethoven, playing trios, quartets, quintets, while Isabel Lowell sat at her piano in the wide living room of their Concord house, her children surrounding her, her lovely head poised at attention, her fingers all energy, all sympathy, upon the keys.

Concord, traditional home of letters, had indeed become, with the Lowell family as core, a source for the cult of music. Each June when school doors closed, teachers arrived from far as well as near to attend the festival conducted by Thomas Whitney Surette, director of music in the schools of Boston, to listen to his admonitions in the cause of musical instruction, to become familiar with the classic folk tunes from various lands, which he had arranged, to listen to such gay and poignant meters as those of the Brahms *liebeslieder* that touch the heart, and to join in a dramatic farewell to the festival by singing Bach chorales as praise to the Almighty, as praise also to the renewal of summer.

Another friend, fortuitously entering in intimacy the scene of my present life, and a figure in a girlhood dream, was Germaine Porel, the daughter of Réjane the actress. We had met in Paris when I was young but then only as the daughters of our respective mothers, come together to chat, in the French manner, amicably but briefly of *la vie:*

> *Ah, c'est la vie, Madame.*
> *Oui, Madame, c'est la vie.*

These lines from a long poem in the repertory of Madame Réjane were supposedly spoken by two children masquerading as grownups. I knew the poem well, having learned it at the behest of my instructress in diction during the winter when I first met Germaine. On another, later, trip to Paris after my marriage, I had gone to see Réjane in her last play, *La Vierge Folle.* This had proved to be so moving, her role so poignantly enacted, that I left the theater barely able to conceal my tears. The following morning, however, I had sufficiently recovered to set out, with the theater program as guide, for the shop on the Boulevard de la Madeleine known as Les Trois Quartiers. There I purchased six pairs of beige-colored gloves with scalloped edges,—at that moment of my life things were measured usually by the dozen or half dozen,—gloves such as Mme. Réjane was wearing in her current play. Then, returning from Europe, at a ladies' luncheon to which I'd been invited, I was accosted by a Mrs. Philip Wilson, wife of an orthopaedic surgeon currently practicing in Boston.

"You were Gladys Rice," she said, taking my hand in hers. "I met you in Paris years ago with my mother, Mme. Réjane. I recognized you at once when you entered the room because of the gloves you were wearing. These were the gloves she preferred to all others."

The conductor of the symphony orchestra who became established in Boston during the years that followed the first war was Pierre Monteux, the Frenchman. His was at first an arduous task, for several of the musicians, in addition to Dr. Muck, had seemed of dubious loyalty and had had to be dropped from the ranks. This, along with depleted numbers, created a lowering of morale. It was as if a tidal wave had receded, hollowing portions of the terrain, spreading devastation across the contours of the map. Little by little, the hollows were filled so that Monteux was able at last to display his admirable skill, and with his rigid disciplinary tactics, plus his sense of dynamic balance, he imparted a fresh impetus to the orchestra, making of it the fluid, forceful, pliant vehicle it has been ever since.

During the five years of his tenure we became friends and I was now and then permitted to attend private rehearsals. I was particularly faithful while the practice period for *Le Sacre du Printemps* was in progress. This early work of Stravinsky had not yet been heard in the United States and a great deal hinged on the *première*. A formidable and most meticulous preparation ensued, a practice toward perfection more detailed and thorough than any I had conceived. Certainly, in my own fiddle work during all the days and weeks and months since my eighth year when music practice had begun, I had not known patience and care as these qualities were spread before me now. I was learning what it meant to repeat with docility and fervor ten or a dozen measures many times over, so many times that they became a part of the individual player's pulse beat, to absorb fearful intricacies, harshly breaking rhythms, until they ran as smoothly as the engine of a great ocean liner. The sound of Monteux's baton tapping the edge of the music stand, rapping to interrupt progress in order to repeat a phrase, became the order of the moment, and it was difficult to believe, as I heard his voice, scolding, pleading with the patient band of men beneath him, that presently, on a certain Friday afternoon, the music would issue free and sure in the way the composer had intended.

The performance, when it came, brought a glorious outpouring of welded sound which captivated a large proportion of the audience, although a few were outraged by its tone of dissonance. During the pause dividing the two halves of Stravinsky's score, I watched Monteux with amusement as he stood, square, stolid, immobile, back to the audience, waiting for the old ladies and gentlemen among the subscribers to gather up hats, coats, umbrellas, canes, and make their obviously protesting way from the hall.

One more encounter behind the scenes came with the rehearsal of an orchestral composition written by Germaine Tailleferre, a young woman who was one of a group of French composers known as *Les Six*. Others in this group were men who had already made important names: Milhaud, Auric, Honegger, Poulenc. Because she was the only woman among them my heart went out in loyalty to Germaine Tailleferre and I looked forward to her success with Boston audiences. She had lately married the publicist Ralph Barton, who, we were told, delighted in his new French wife's manner of industry and thrift. His previous wives had looked overkindly upon the luxuries: capes of silver fox, mink coats, elegant concoctions of every sort, whereas Germaine, when not busy with musical composition, cut and stitched her own clothes. She preferred the results of such handiwork to the highly priced garments to be had in Paris, a new experience to the world of glamour and wealth.

The final rehearsal of the Tailleferre composition was called on the evening that preceded the Friday concert, and several of the composer's friends were invited to attend. We arrived to group ourselves about her, all save Ralph Barton who had been detained in New York. It was rumored that he would presently arrive in the company of Charlie Chaplin, an old friend. Halfway through the rehearsal the two entered, most conspicuously in the vast, empty hall, and within minutes the musicians were keeping but one eye on the notes of the score while the other was fixed upon Chaplin. Monteux, back to the hall, was not himself tempted but he must have been aware that his men lacked the convincing attitude toward their work. Later, when he set the baton down, he was drawn into conversation with the comedian whose charm pervaded the place, insidious as perfume, and I was unhappy for the modest young composer demoted thus to second place.

More or less continuously between the births of my four children, I studied violin with Professor Felix Winternitz, who gave, in addition to daily hours at the Conservatory, private lessons at his brick, swell-fronted house on Hemenway Street. Clad in wide, open-collared shirt, corduroy jacket and leather-thonged sandals, he dealt with recalcitrance, inertia, stupidity, one pupil leaving, another arriving, as the slow hours moved with them. Now and then he may have been heartened because of some passage played with perfection, some minor technical point well achieved, but the cast of the passing day, monotonous, drab, much resembled the colors run together in a child's box of paints. To offset perennial lackluster from without, he encouraged an inner life, secret but strong. A philosopher by instinct, later by necessity, he dwelt on the wisdom of Spinoza, and during the winter that he first encountered Spengler's *Decline of the West* he was doubly preoccupied. This book absorbed him, and at my lessons there appeared an added quality of detachment, even sorrow, in his aspect, which I looked upon with respect.

Now and then, at the end of the hour of instruction, Mr. Winternitz asked to be permitted to escort me home. We set out sometimes in rain or snow and on the doorstep were startled at the sound from an upper window of Frau Winternitz's strident German voice calling: *"Vater!* You have your overshoes *vergessen!"*

We walked slowly along the quiet streets that surround the Mother Church of the Christian Scientists and our conversation dwelt upon the deeper verities. He tried to make me understand the tenets and the methodology of Spengler, tried to draw me toward that remote world where were the haunting presence of gloom and the acceptance of despair: factors not easily accessible to my nature. Not easy to accept even the pace at which I moved beside my teacher, who, violin case in hand, was impeded not alone by his thought but by a limping gait also. His limp was due to an accident suffered while deer hunting soon after his arrival in the United States. He was then a young man, an Austrian violin virtuoso, who counted on establishing his name among top soloists. An intimate of Fritz Kreisler, together they had studied with the great Auer and begun their careers almost simultaneously. The shooting accident in the woods of Maine, when a companion mistook Winternitz for legitimate prey, brought an enduring distortion to finger and leg, brought also an inevitable end to the career of virtuoso. Impossible, he realized with finality, to limp his entrance onto the stage, to exhibit the bow hand, one finger shot away.

The philosopher was born at that moment of pain, of grief, and of the long patience which is the order of life renewed. In process of this renewal he had come to resemble some Buddha nourished on contemplation, and probably it did not occur to him that the surroundings in Hemenway Street, the homely setting administered by his *Hausfrau* were an uncouth background for metaphysics.

Occasionally the house sprang to life, in the German sense of application to hospitality, when Frau Winternitz served their guests with the substantial foods she had spent the day or days in preparing. One such party I was invited to attend. It was a banquet given in honor of Mischa Elman, who had come to town to play a violin recital on the next day in Symphony Hall. My husband was also invited but I managed to find an excuse which would free him from a situation far removed from the ordinary course of his life and difficult for him to enter with zest. He was kind enough to insist on my going, however, and an hour after our own dinner at home had come to an end, I set out in a taxi for Hemenway Street. Their house in the dark, still street was ablaze, and the hostess, a heavy woman with a genial manner, her cheeks flaming with excitement, let me in at the front door. The men, a group of musicians, were gathered about the guest of honor on the floor above, drinking

their preprandial schnapps, but they were soon summoned to the dining room and placed about a circular table beneath a chandelier of stained glass lit by
strong bulbs. The table was laden with every sort of con-
diment and pickle and jelly. I observed this with dismay,
having so recently eaten another meal, while Frau Winternitz set before us the black bean soup which was to
be the preliminary to four or five more courses.

Notwithstanding this sort of Lucullan tradition in the
matter of food, Winternitz held intact his metaphysical
dreams. Later, when his wife had died and his sons
were established in their careers, he was able to cut the
vestiges of bourgeois ties and go free. He went on voyages across the seas and along the surfaces of the earth,
and his violin was both passport and luggage. He went
bareheaded and in sandaled feet, there being no one to
say him nay. He went to the Orient and he spent long
weeks among the flowering oases of New Zealand, and
in lieu of base, of home, he could rely on the Bach Sonatas for Unaccompanied Violin. These he played long
and lovingly, and, in the pattern of the Pied Piper, he
drew lovers of music as he went. Presently, growing old,
he returned to America and engaged a small room beneath the roof of the Faculty Club at Harvard. From
here he came to pay me visits, to advise, to sustain, with
his belief in a benign providence. He was never hurried
or thrown off balance and he was pleased, with his far-
sighted wisdom, to answer the questions put to him by
those who like myself were more eager than he to bribe
fate into compliance with our designs. He drew toward
his end removed, apparently, from harassment of
thought and spirit, but during these last years he must

have suffered as his strength faded, as he was more and more alone. He needed then the familiar things from which he had earlier chosen to be severed; he needed companionship and care. There are, after all, limits to man's bravery and selflessness, limits which bodily strength must finally confront, dark areas which the human imagination cannot penetrate without meeting the unbearable intensities that bring the end. He died alone in his room beneath the rafters and I was not there to wish him Godspeed.

Another Boston character who courted wisdom as companion, a being less selfless, more fortunate, perhaps, than my violin teacher but equally apart from the pedestrian conformities, was Mrs. Jack Gardner. I knew her first as a member of a luncheon club composed of various ladies older than I who had kindly invited me to join them. Each was distinguished in her own way, and I, but a youthful bride, was rather shy. Looking back on those gatherings, I fear the others must have been disappointed in me, a new and callow member, found me deficient in the qualities they had imputed to a foreigner from the far land of New York. Possibly they hoped by my presence to instill new and younger blood into their midst, to disrupt an over-homogeneous point of view, an attitude grown weary from too long association. But there was not enough of me, not sufficient courage in my heart nor stamina nor plain everyday knowledge, to set contrary currents in motion. I remember my confusion when Mrs. Gardner from across the table, measuring me with an eye which seemed to be not entirely friendly, asked for my ideas on the education of the young.

"Heavens! I have no ideas at all!" would have been the answer given to one of my own generation, to one less august than she who questioned me now. As it was, it behooved me to be clever, original, to summon the appearance of plausibility. Whether, when I spoke at last, my words flung against the silence of the lunch table, whether my pronouncement was of any value, I cannot remember. Mrs. Gardner, I noticed, smiled when I had done, my cheeks flaming to match the braised tomato on my plate, and when in future we met, her eye which had once coldly measured held a gleam of kindness tied to amusement. Pity for innocence and youth may well have been the feeling I had aroused in her.

With this question put by Mrs. Gardner as springboard, my ideas on the education of the young unfolded now, to become, little by little, an important factor in my existence and that of my children. Eventually when the youthful class based on the tenets of John Dewey outgrew our living room on Commonwealth Avenue and was moved to a loft on Chestnut Street above the shop of Gebelein, silversmith; when, in turn, the children who were gathered here multiplied in years and numbers so that the little Beaver School became the Beaver Country Day School in Chestnut Hill, then truly I might have answered Mrs. Gardner's question with understanding.

At Mrs. Gardner's palace, Fenway Court, on the days open to the public, it interested me to watch its owner. Dressed inconspicuously, in a manner calculated to blend with the background, like some shadow cast by a minor cloud that temporarily obscures the sun, she came and went among the crowd. She wished not to be recognized by her friends, to remain unremarked, a fellow explorer among others, while she listened and observed, deriving amusement and gratification and sustenance from the behavior and enthusiasm of the crowd. Once I had a glimpse of her, hair drawn severely back under a cloche hat, large pearl earrings the one ornament to her plain white face, while, fitted into an embrasure rather above the level of sightseers, she appeared in the classic posture of a gargoyle. She might have been looking down upon the torpid waters of the river Seine from a niche on the façade of Notre Dame. It seemed difficult then to reconcile this uncouth figure with the erstwhile charmer of men, hostess to the great, famous for the knowledge and skill with which she had assembled her enduring collection of painting, sculpture, interiors. Difficult to think of her as the possessor of those letters displayed in rows of glass-covered cases nearby, letters written her by world figures, or to associate her with the great boisterous painting by John Sargent, the "Carmencita," symbol of zest and vitality, flaunting its sensuous appeal close to the cloistered court below, where in exotic brilliance grew acacia, lilies, calceolarias and the joyous flowers of spring.

A day came, following an interval of years, when I was summoned to call on Mrs. Gardner who lay prostrate on a narrow bed in a great room at the top of her palace. Her mind functioned as of old, untouched by the paralysis which had felled her body, and she continued to receive her friends, talking with them, unlike most who grow old, of the present rather than the past. She lay unadorned, a little shrunken woman with eyes of an intensity one could not forget and a smile wherein a certain wistfulness blended with the sharp penetration of other years. She had latterly been distributing her personal belongings to youthful members of the Gardner family, laying bare the jewel box holding the famous rope of pearls which had, in the Sargent portrait, encircled her waist: stripping herself, like some novice become a nun, of worldly paraphernalia, worldly concern. I thought of one of the early queens of France, Blanche of Castille, Margaret of Provence, preparing to meet her God.

From me, Mrs. Gardner wished to hear of my violin, of the concerts I had recently heard. She asked my ideas on the skill of various instrumental virtuosi now before the public. I described my first years of violin study in Boston when I had journeyed out to Medfield beyond the Blue Hill Reservation in order to take lessons of Charles Loeffler, that excellent musician and friend of hers for whom I was eventually unable to work because of the difference in our attitudes, our temperaments, his and mine. He was an artist who strove for a dimension beyond that brought by a direct appeal to the senses. He labored for purity, the thin clear line aimed at celestial spaces. Yet, for a student such as I, the process was painful and the step halting. The act of teaching me must have been painful also for him, and as he sat listening to my performance, withdrawn, wrapped in the lucubrations of his own mind, the horsehair of my bow as I drew it along the catgut of strings seemed to emit something indelicate in that rarefied air, and I felt myself a gross, untutored creature insufficiently removed from earth's primordial slime. So, one day, with a new baby as valid excuse for suspending lessons, I dropped the trips to Medfield and never returned.

All this I recounted to Mrs. Gardner while her eyes were fixed upon me in reflection. Presently she uttered the name of Povla Frijsh, Danish singer, a protégée in Boston of Mr. Loeffler whose songs were a part of her repertoire. Hers had been a notable example of temperament retrained, a quality of voice made over. Deliberately, the story was, this singer had molded anew the timbre of the vocal cords in order to formulate the cool yet sustained tone needed for the rendering of Loeffler's music, the chill, steady reflection of the moon on a frosty night. Curious it had been to observe carefully contrived restraint in an eager, passionate woman, blond hair braided heavily about her head, arms framed in floating gray chiffon, heroine of a Norse saga. Yet one respected her courage in denying herself reliance on honeyed sound while she gave an interpretation of the notes that was so just, so comprehensive, so pure, as to carry all before it.

An evening of music had taken place not many days back, I now told Mrs. Gardner, when some of us were invited to a song recital at the house of a friend, a beautiful house overlooking the Public Garden. Povla Frijsh was to sing.

"It was one of the most wonderful evenings of my life," I exclaimed, and the smile given me by Mrs. Gardner made me happy for us both. She herself, I well knew, had been blessed with many such evenings earned through the countless favors she had scattered with wide gesture.

"Spring was in the air," I continued, "the peepers made a great racket, the maple buds were beginning to cluster on the trees in the garden, and the moon was out full. The music room, almost bare and very elegant, was decorated with masses of Roman anemones, and a fire burned on the hearth. There were only eight or ten of us there, our hostess wanting to make sure of concentrated attention from her guests, wanting Mme. Frijsh to be as much at home as we, her audience, were bound to be. Nothing forced, everything spontaneous. And it *was* like that."

"How did the quality of her voice strike you on that evening?" Mrs. Gardner asked.

"There was no separating the quality from the effect of the whole. It was all of one piece, a unit, a unit of beauty. She sang like an angel. Youthful freshness was not there, I suppose—I hadn't heard her in earlier years—but her skill and her magical control overwhelmed us. And the warmth within her grew as the hearth fire blazed in that perfect setting which she herself felt, of course, along with our great pleasure. So that tied to her natural charm and her lovely appearance, dressed in slim black, a sprig of mimosa pinned over her heart, she gave us the ultimate—more dream than reality."

Mrs. Gardner lay, white and silent, and I stopped short as I spoke those last words. I did not wish to tire her, and after all, what is there beyond the ultimate, beyond a fair dream? I moved in my chair preparatory to bidding her good-by. She looked at me as if to ask a question based on far immensities. I paused for a moment but the question was not spoken.

"Good-by," I said slowly, taking her hand in mine, attempting with that gesture to bring her the reality she may have been trying to find.

12

YEARS OF WAR

Washington during the First World War lost its gentle air of the provincial and, overnight, stretched its fingertips to reach the farthermost spaces of the globe. Thus it became a chameleon, vivid in its changing hues, compelling, astir as an ant heap crawling with life, a mill grinding the lives of lowly civil servants, grinding the minds of those who directed action from high places, a slough of despair to any engaged with the repercussions of death, happy opportunity for the social-loving element among well-placed individuals. For me, it was a fairyland strewn with glittering particles of treasure to be gathered without effort. I felt, I suppose, as had the forty-niners of California: bright gold lay in the palm of my hand.

My husband had engaged himself for the war with the Department of the Navy, and his work on the staff of Admiral Sims held him alternately with headquarters at Washington and London. I was the mother of three small children. I was young and eager and not sorry, for the moment, to have gone from Boston, the Boston of which for six years I had been a part and where my children were born, a Boston irremediably and quite properly engaged at present in folding gauze for bandages, in organizing drives for the benefit of the Red Cross and the Liberty Loan, in gathering garments for refugees from disaster in distant lands. In Washington, although these wartime pursuits, these aids to combat, were carried on also, they constituted but a small part of the whole and were almost obscured by the life of glamour that floated airily at the summit.

Now and then, as I woke into one more gleaming Washington day, my conscience smote me. What right had I to so intense an enjoyment of pleasure during this period of wide suffering? What of the battle fronts of France and Africa: bodies rotting beneath the sun, gory trenches where men's limbs lay scattered like broken glass in a junkyard, bloodstained meadows of a countryside once fecund with oats and wheat? Yet my own life persisted, bringing the certainty of days unrolling to infinity, days fertile with new knowledge, new awareness, new happiness.

One early morning in January as I lay thinking of these things, there was a knock on my bedroom door and a maid entered carrying my breakfast tray. She closed the window, pulled wide the taffeta curtains, placed the tray across my knees in the great four-poster bed with its ruffle-trimmed canopy. At one corner of the tray stood a small package and in her hand she held another, larger one.

"What are these, Ellen?" I asked.

"They were brought by the orderly of Colonel the

Honorable Arthur Murray, Madam," she answered.
"The Colonel sent his regards."

"Oh, how kind!" I said. "And it's a lovely day again,
isn't it?"

"Yes, Madam, it is. Almost spring weather. A light-
weight suit will do for you today."

"Thank you, Ellen. Will you ask the little girls to come
in and say good-by before they go to their class and tell
Freda she can bring the baby down whenever she
likes?"

"Yes, Madam, I will."

Before pouring my coffee I reached out to touch the
package on the tray. I loved the excitement connected
with the unwrapping of presents, untying the string,
loosening the paper, coming at last on the hidden object
chosen with care by someone who wished me well.
Rather than prolong expectation I opened it at once,
to find a circular metal container of cigarettes from
Dunhill in London, and with pleasure I thought back
on an evening recently when, at a grandiose party given
by Mrs. Evalyn Walsh, owner of the fabulous Hope Dia-
mond, I had gone out to dinner on the arm of Colonel
Murray. He had immediately become a benefactor, protecting me from the pressures of the unfamiliar, helping
to serve me artichoke and guinea hen from the silver
salvers in the hands of flunkeys, talking to me of the
books he had read, his voice steady and quiet against the
crescendos of babbling voices about us. Glancing at him
sidewise from my confined position at the dinner table,
I thought him the most engaging of men with his carefully cut features and tidy black mustache, his dress uniform of the British army, a clanking sword at his side.

And now, alone, confronting my morning tray, the magic sprang up once again. Here was a generous supply of the cigarettes he had offered me from his silver case at that first meeting, and here in the larger package was a book of essays by Augustine Birrell, a man whom Colonel Murray much admired.

A fortunate woman I was. I had begun to find this out afresh on the instant of our arrival in Washington to occupy the pleasant house belonging to the famous eye specialist, Dr. Wilmer, at the corner of Fourteenth and R Streets, and so carefully selected for our comfort by my husband. We had brought from Boston the servants accustomed to waiting on us, including the superior Norwegian nursemaid who looked after the children.

Our two little girls, Betsy and Priscilla, had reached nursery school age, and, with several parents among our friends, I had helped to organize a class in the neighborhood to which they went each weekday morning. Betsy, who as the eldest showed a certain precocity in growing up, was later given her first lessons in horseback riding, and when spring came, she and I rode out together along the bridle paths of Rock Creek Park, ambling slowly, allowing our horses to canter on level ground, smelling the sweetness of honeysuckle, hearing the murmur of the stream. My small boy, Jock, was growing well. Indeed, the air of Washington appeared to agree with them all, including my husband who walked each morning to his office in the Navy Department and thoroughly enjoyed his work. An atmosphere of well being pervaded the house, making it a pleasant background not only for us but for the friends who came there.

In the drawing room stood a grand piano, and there,

one long afternoon following another, I played violin and piano sonatas with Tom Spring-Rice, nephew of the British Ambassador. People came and went, the little girls wandered in to lie on the floor, a few devotees lingered into the twilight listening to Mozart, Schubert, Brahms, Vivaldi and César Franck, forgetting perhaps, as Tom and I forgot, that across the water men were dying in wanton slaughter even while the lovely sequences fell in innocence and purity upon the ear. My husband, because of his work, was closer than I to the rigors of war, but he seemed proud of my musical flowering and it pleased him to listen for a while when at evening he returned home.

Of Tom Spring-Rice I became as fond as of a brother turned mentor. He was tall, a trifle stooped and near-sighted, while his sparse hair was always rumpled. He belonged to that race of Englishmen who were made of genius and modesty, who possessed humor joined to the tragic sense: a Lear or a Lewis Carroll. His knowledge of music was complete, his erudition immense, his taste impeccable. His memory extended far and deep so that he was able to play without the aid of printed notes from Bach's *Well-Tempered Clavier* and much of the *Art of the Fugue*. For Brahms he had a special love and he persuaded me to play the two sonatas written for clarinet by the master in his latter years, his inspiration sprung from the sounds of daily practice made by a clarinetist living next door. Lovely, rollicking sounds they were, alternating with a protracted sadness like the alternations of water in a sunny spring brook and the lull brought it by a widening of the stream beneath the shade of downward drooping branches.

Tom and I played the Clarinet Sonata in E-Flat Major, arranged for violin, at an evening music party given by Mary Howe, the composer, and there, on this particular evening, I met Nigel Law, a young secretary of the British Embassy, a man who was to remain a lifelong friend. He was drawn to me then, he later said, by the intensity with which I concentrated on the performance, like a schoolgirl determined to remember the words of her valedictory piece for graduation day, and by the fluttering of the freesia spray pinned to my bodice betraying the agitated pounding of my heart.

I hoped, when I was told of this, that it might also have been the tone of the violin that attracted Nigel Law, the sound of it blending with the clarity of the piano passages under the capable fingers of Tom Spring-Rice. The violin itself, the instrument I played on, was that particular Stradivarius known as the Avery Strad and given me not long since by my husband. It was a splendid instrument loftily replacing the fiddle of my girlhood, a Guadagnini of lesser fame. The bow that I used on the strings of the Stradivarius, there in Washington, was a particularly fine one designed by the celebrated French maker, François Tourte, at Paris in the year 1780. This we had selected together, my husband and I, on a trip to England after the birth of my first child. It had come from Bond Street in London, from Hill, purveyor extraordinary of musical instruments to the world. Many were the professional musicians who, over the years, envied me the possession of this bow. Among them was Paul Kochanski, the great Polish violinist, who said to me, "I know that the Tourte bow you will not sell to me now, *chère Madame,* but I beg of you kindly to leave it to me in your will."

He kissed my hand to further this request, but I found it difficult to promise any such deed. I was rather embarrassed for the moment. This awkwardness might well have been tempered to charity had I been able to foresee that he was himself to die a few years later.

Another focal point for the making of music in Washington was the house of the Nicholas Longworths. Here, at evening, Alice Longworth assembled their friends, dining them, wining them, so that, as the mounting hours slipped toward a new day, they might listen, docile and content, in the semi-obscurity of her living room to the performance on his violin of her husband and the fellow musicians he gathered about him, virtuosi such as Heifetz or Zimbalist, alternating with the lesser accomplishment of eager amateurs. The qualification, the standard for admission to the ranks, was none other than the ability to render the sound of chamber music in understandable fashion. The degree of perfection mattered not so much as an awareness of the composer's intention.

Apart from the pleasures of music making, the instruction given me by Tom Spring-Rice, the flattering attentions of Arthur Murray, there was another element of Washington existence not vouchsafed to me during the Boston prewar years. This was the renewed presence of Henry Adams, settled "for the duration," or for as long as the rest of the globe was forbidden him, in his house at 1607 H Street, a landmark at the corner of Lafayette Square. Next door had lived his friend John Hay, and across the way Mrs. Cameron had held her salon when she was young and beautiful and a magnet for the world

of men. They had all been in love with her, with her
Titian hair and the caustic wit which had so often in-
timidated me in the days of my travels with her in Europe. They enjoyed the vivid sparkle of her mind, like
quartz glinting; they succumbed to her feminine charm
and her kindness to those whom she singled out to be-
friend. It was Mrs. Cameron—General Sherman's niece,
and hostess on her arrival in Washington to another
uncle, Senator Sherman—who had formed a close bond
with Mr. and Mrs. Henry Adams when first she became
the bride of the elderly Senator Cameron from Pennsyl-
vania. She had nursed and nurtured Uncle Henry after
his wife's sudden and startling death, and now, although
she had renounced the United States as a dwelling place,
she continued nonetheless in close communication with
him.

At present, in this period of war, living in the house
at H Street, helping Uncle Henry to entertain his many
guests, was the charming Aileen Tone, a friend of his
Hooper nieces. Aileen was beautiful and gentle and
clever, and, best of all, she was able to beguile him
away, like David with Saul, from the dark places de-
ployed about his tragic sense. She sang to him as he
sat in a low chair beside the piano listening to her soft,
untutored voice while she hummed the melodies composed by those who lived and loved during that twelfth
century which he had made so entirely his own:

Ah, ma belle qui m'a désolé. . . .

Often I lingered at Uncle Henry's side, bound to him
by the tender beauty of the words we heard together, by
the line of melody rising clear and poignant to deepen

their meaning. I lingered beside him wondering whence came his initial despair, wondering what he saw in the distance that so overwhelmed him: distrust, disappointment, dislike of the current world, the greed, the strife, the crude unfeeling of the average man? The average man, all men, he turned from more and more, from their blatant stupidities, their monotonous ineptitude; gross, dumb creatures they appeared to him, plotting for the destruction of the world. His trust, his love, he gave with open hand and with wide gesture to the Virgin, bright core of his existence, the Virgin who with grace and dignity occupied her throne at Chartres. In lesser degree he gave his confidence and affection to those nieces who possessed a little of his Lady's innocence, her knowledge of joy and sorrow. And so I was allowed to sit at his side to share with him the wisdom that instructed.

During the months that passed I was able now and then to amuse Uncle Henry with tales of my worldly doings, accounts of the parties I attended with my husband when he was at home, without him when he was in London.

"Last evening, Uncle Henry," I began one day, "there was a quite marvelous party at Mrs. Marshall Field's."

"Marvelous, my child?"

"Well—unusual, if you like."

"An old lady of vitality."

"And imagination too. She telephoned several weeks back to say she had been told of the Alice in Wonderland party that some of us had given when I was Alice and Nigel Law was the March Hare and Ronnie Campbell was the Dormouse. You heard of it, didn't you? My costume was quite perfect, I think, because three or four of the young men from the Embassy had gone along to help me select the material for it. As I wasn't born in England they believed I might not buy the right thing. They chose a good serviceable muslin, suitable for growing girls, and Cash's red braid to trim the skirt. I might have bought black velvet for the trim, they said. 'Too swank and not washable.'" I smiled at the memory of this pleasant business. "And Mrs. Field had also heard of our charades, those the English secretaries enter into with so much gusto."

"A clever lot, those young men. But that does not necessarily portend good things for their future." He shook his head as if watching the precipitate gathering of storm clouds.

"Well, Mrs. Field asked if I would collect Nigel and Ronnie and Jock Balfour and Tom Spring-Rice and so on, plus Mrs. Truxton Beale and Mr. Henry White, people who would enter into the spirit, and invite them to dine at her house. She had an engagement to dine elsewhere that evening, she said, but she planned to return between ten-thirty and eleven and wanted the charade to be in full swing."

"Imagination there, as you say."

"Yes."

"And it took place?"

"Last night. A great success. And so grand! Mrs. Field's butler telephoned yesterday morning to inquire whether the dinner table was to be set with the gold or silver service. I chose the silver."

"A pity. Why not have the best? More becoming to your appearance too."

"But the idea of gold seemed so Arabian Nights, all that splendor. Anyway, Nigel Law thought up a quite perfect word for the charade just before the clock struck ten-thirty, and the others did some superb acting, particularly Ronnie Campbell who played Isadora Duncan doing a barefoot dance. He took off his shoes and socks and put a trailing scarf around his shoulders. *So* funny, over his long tails. How we laughed!"

"I can imagine. And Mrs. Field?"

"She timed her entrance perfectly. We were going full steam ahead. She was as amused as all the rest of us."

"You've put her on the map."

"Oh, Uncle Henry. What a thing to say! One of the famous hostesses of Washington. And I like her. She's friendly and gay. At the moment, though, she's rather sad because the Italian chef who's been with her for so long has given notice. He wants to leave for the reason that on the evenings she's at home alone, once a week perhaps, she orders nothing but a baked apple. Not enough of his skill needed for that."

"Poor woman. What tragedy!"

I laughed and Uncle Henry seemed almost amused and Aileen, coming into the room, smiled her smile of happy complicity.

Aileen I had known a short while before our entrance into the war. The first meeting took place at Beverly Cove in our summer house on a wooded hill overlooking Massachusetts Bay. My baby boy was little more than a week old, and I lay in bed tended by a nurse, surrounded by flowers, facing an open fire that took the chill from a gusty day in April. Uncle Henry was announced from belowstairs. Hastily, the nurse smoothed my hair

and brought me my prettiest bed jacket, but still I felt
that the years which had intervened between this and
my last meeting with him in Paris six years earlier must
have left their mark on my appearance. It was in Paris
that Uncle Henry had cautioned me not to throw myself
away on the first young man who might care to marry
me, and already I had become the mother of three children.

He entered presently with Aileen: the same small
bearded figure of alacrity, of shy approach, of potential
acrimony, of affection obliquely bestowed. The nurse
had placed two chairs beside the bed and my visitors
faced a painting on the wall beyond, one that represented
a group of Chinese porcelains standing on a walnut bureau, a water color by Walter Gay which I had recently
bought. The Gays were warm friends of Uncle Henry,
and their lovely Paris apartment overlooking a garden
on the Left Bank was hung with the portraits of the
great Clouet. Mrs. Cameron had several times taken
Elizabeth Hoyt and me to see the Gays, and we had
lunched with them at their country house where the
splendor of environment and interior remained in my
mind rather less than did the quality of the *gâteau St.
Honoré* fabricated in their kitchen by their pastry chef.
To be able to command a performance such as this in
one's own house seemed a quite marvelous feat. The
Gays had been intimate friends also of Henry James,
and I had heard with interest their account of his last
visit to New York where, walking south on Fifth Avenue toward Madison Square, he had partially covered his
eyes with his hand that they might be protected from
the sight of the Flatiron Building. The sharply incisive

lines of its silhouette against the sky acted like the thrust
of a rapier upon his sensibilities, they said. It had never
affected me in that way when I walked by. In fact I had
always liked its slim, triangular thrust upward. But, I
reflected, I was not a famous author in need of being
shielded from the possible ill effects of distaste.

Glancing at Uncle Henry now, I saw that his eyes were
on the painting.

"There is Walter Gay's interior of a corner in their
Paris salon, Aileen," he said. "The *potiches* on the com-
mode I know well. Hawthorn blue. I remember the day
he bought them at the auction sale of a well-known col-
lector. Very fine."

Before leaving, Uncle Henry spoke of the prospects
of the coming Congressional election in which my husband was running on the Republican ticket.

"Victory or defeat, you must make a point of coming
to Washington," he had said.

Now here I was, in Washington, going often to lunch
or to tea in the house planned for him by H. H. Richard-
son, a large bland house of stone and brick. Climbing
the wide staircase, I usually found Uncle Henry in the
living room above the entrance where chairs were low
as if for some game to be played upon the floor, where
the rugs, the great vases of porcelain, the bronzes, told
the story of Henry Adams's pleasure in the Far East,
where the sun came across the square to fall on the water colors of the English school that lined the walls,
where, beyond wide portiere doors, was the dining room
with its half-light and the Turner oils that one forgot to
remember, so lively was the conversation at the center
table.

There came the morning when Aileen summoned me, as often she was apt to do, a summons for the same day. "Uncle Henry has an important question to put to you," she said. "Won't you come to lunch?"

I arrived early and went to sit on a stool at Uncle Henry's feet, my usual position. A glass of sherry was in my hands and I sipped it looking anxiously upward. In spite of our intimacy and the passing of the years, I continued to feel in his presence a schoolgirl's awe of the teacher who controls and shapes her mind.

"It occurs to me," he said, crossing one knee above the other, staring out beyond the window, "that you may not be able to distinguish between an English gentleman and an English bounder. Differences here subtle enough to escape the notice of one not versed in them."

I followed the direction of Uncle Henry's gaze, dwelling for a while upon distant treetops as I dwelt also on an answer to this question, one never put to me before, one I had not yet considered.

"I'm not sure, Uncle Henry, but I rather think I do. Is a bounder apt to wear spats and carry a gold-headed cane?" My thoughts flew to a man I had briefly met, member of one of the numerous British war missions now in Washington.

Uncle Henry chuckled. "You are on the right track, 'getting warm,' as the children say, playing twenty questions."

"And a bounder doesn't care for charades and has never heard of Edward Lear or the *Jumblies*."

"I can see that your instinct is a reliable one, my dear. Mind you don't swerve from it. Plenty of women have. The dashing looks, the hair pomade, the assiduous manner, mislead them. A fatal business."

"Better to have tousled, dust-colored hair like Tom's, Tom Spring-Rice." I laughed.

"Far better," he answered, and patted the top of my head.

This was my last meeting with Henry Adams. The next summons from Aileen came at eight-thirty in the morning a week later.

"Gladys, dear," her soft voice spoke through the telephone, "come at once, if you will. Uncle Henry is dead."

"Uncle Henry, dead?"

"He died in the night, full of peace. We didn't discover it until this morning."

"Oh, Aileen—"

"Yes, dear. And now, if you wish to see him, to see splendor such as to be remembered always, you will come."

"I will come. I'll come right away."

I dressed and went to the house and on up to the front bedroom at the top of the house. There, in a wide bed beneath the high ceiling, Uncle Henry lay forever still, a warrior resting in carved stone on his tomb. I stood beside Aileen, holding her hand, and I looked down upon his face wherein the accumulated strength and sorrow and serenity of a deeply felt life was bared to us as it had not been when he existed on earth, when the outward, superficial exchanges of the day-to-day scene intervened to blur the verities. For, wrapping Henry Adams's small round body, his jocose manner, his fluttering gesture, there had been a mask of concealment, a mask almost puerile, born in withdrawal out of shyness and pride, established in order that the world might have no hint of the ferment, the fury, of his spirit. Here in death the spirit was visible at last—a final compliance bringing the final nobility.

I left Uncle Henry forever on a warm morning in March of 1918 when the cherry trees from Japan were preparing to open their flowers once more along the banks of the Potomac. These he would not know again, but neither was he to know of the German bomb presently to fall on the Church of St. Gervais in Paris: one more blow, like those earlier ones, perpetrated upon France, which had struck deep at his vulnerable heart. He was buried on Holy Saturday beside his wife in Rock Creek Park, beneath the figure carved to her memory by Saint-Gaudens, the brooding figure that represents fate.

A few weeks later, following the Armistice, I received a wire that summoned me to my mother's bedside. Mamma, also, had been touched by fate's all-encompassing hand, and was drifting, now, swiftly on her way from the world of the flesh. At last I had become intimate with death, staring it in the face, trying to realize its import, trying to recognize the melancholy game of its playing, a game wherein the losing card was dealt to me. The years of war had come to an end.

13

LABOR AND LOVE

A SMALL voice woke me before dawn, a small hand on my face. "Mummy, that man doesn't let me sleep."

"What?" I asked of the darkness and sudden new reality.

"He talks all the time, Mummy."

I stretched out an arm to turn on the light, to see Jean, my four-year-old, barefoot, nightie clinging to her slim form. "Who talks?" I asked.

"The man in the nursery."

Then I remembered. It was Hugh Walpole, the English novelist and lecturer, come on the previous day armed with letters of introduction. We had invited him to spend the night in our apartment at 191 Commonwealth Avenue, where our four children and the servants occupied all available bedrooms. Only the day nursery with its divan against the wall held space for an occasional guest. Two of the children's rooms flanked it on either side.

"Here, get into bed with me, my pet," I said. Soon we

slept in happy proximity.

Next morning, a pink-cheeked, well-nourished author came to breakfast in apologetic mood. He hoped, he said, that he had not wakened the household with his performance during the night.

"I'm a poor sleeper and the thought of my pending Boston lecture made me nervous. I spoke a good deal of it aloud as I paced the floor, a bad habit, I fear."

On another night, a pajama-clad small boy wandered sleepily into the living room to be taken into his mother's lap as together they listened to Robert Schmitt, French pianist. At the close of his recital in Jordan Hall earlier that evening, the musician had come to our apartment for late supper and, cigar in mouth, sat at the concert-sized Steinway in a room that stretched the width of the building, as he pounded out the triumphant sequences of Bach's A-Minor Fugue. My son Jock, not yet seven years old, already conversant with music of a superior quality, had been aroused by the sound and had come to participate at close quarters.

My children were accustomed to seeing and hearing the musicians who arrived at the house, often to play with me the piano parts of the various violin sonatas. One, an older lady, wife of a Harvard professor, was a fine, serious pianist. Another was a pretty girl who played with passionate accuracy, with difficulty holding at bay the suitors who strove to wean her from the long hours of practice. There was also the youth, later to become a composer, who was then working for his degree at Harvard. He was shy and unable to communicate easily with his fellow creatures. But seated before the ivory and ebony keys of a piano, the dam opened and water flowed full and free. His musical sense was balanced and sure. We were a mutually sympathetic team.

At the end of the afternoon, it was the young man's habit to stand politely and to utter the same stiff phrase: "I enjoyed that very much."

"So did I."

"I hope you'll be able to play with me again soon."

"What about next Wednesday at four?" I asked, as usual.

"I'd like to. Thank you." And he was gone.

Once, at the close of this customary exchange, he added a sentence I had not before heard.

"I'm afraid I can't make it Wednesday. I have an exam."

"Some other day, then," I answered casually.

That evening, on the telephone, the young man's father spoke to me. "I understand that my son has broken next Wednesday's appointment with you."

"Yes. He spoke of an examination."

"If you've not yet made other plans you may count on his being there."

"And the exam?"

"I don't care a fig for that. No exam can equal in importance the fact that he's made a friend. You are probably the one person with whom he's able to carry on a conversation."

"Not a very extensive one." I laughed. "But he's a real musician and we do manage to communicate."

"Wednesday at four, as usual?" the worried parent asked.

"Yes, certainly," I answered.

The children arriving home from school or play were

apt to drop into the living room at the sound of music and on a certain hour of the afternoon my boy Jock sat at the piano, his governess knitting beside him, repeating the exercises and pieces given him by his teacher to prepare. One day I entered to find the governess in a state of irritation.

"I'm sorry to have to tell you that Jock is behaving very badly," she said. "He's playing in heedless fashion, one wrong note after another, no matter what I say."

"I'm *not* playing wrong notes, Mum," the boy said, "but she won't believe me. She doesn't understand Stravinsky."

I glanced over his head at the music to find that he was engaged with those dissonant small pieces of Stravinsky: *Les Cinq Doigts*. Here were five-finger exercises which few untrained musicians might regard as a legitimate part of the day's work. In this case I was able to make an explanation which somewhat assuaged the governess' feelings, but in another case that concerned young Jean, explanation did not serve. I had gone into the nursery to bid the little girl good night and found her in the lap of a nursemaid who sat in a rocking chair keeping time to the rhythm of a lullaby which she sang in a kind of monotone.

"Mummy," said Jean on my entrance, pulling herself straight to make her point clear, "please tell Molly to sing in tune."

This was the child who had made an entrance into the world several weeks ahead of her time, having been jogged into new sensibility by her mother's running, at Symphony Hall, up two flights of marble stairs in order to reach the top balcony before the doors closed on a

Saturday evening performance of Borodin's *Prince Igor.*
Music was her birthright.

The children, I remember, gathered in the living
room, four of them, to see the famous violin known as
the Lord Nelson Strad, when it was briefly unwrapped
by a dealer from overseas, who hoped we might buy it.
Their imaginations were stirred by the story of the great
naval hero who played upon his fiddle during the
pauses between gunfire, taking it from a cupboard in
his cabin on the flagship *Victory* previous to the Battle
of Trafalgar. My eldest, Betsy, asked to be allowed to
hold it in her hands, and Priscilla, her *fides Achates,*
did the same. The younger ones, in the usual pattern,
followed suit, and presently, with the sense of having
conspired with history, they watched the violin as it was
being returned to its case. The Nelson Strad did not become mine—although at the moment my husband had
offered me a fine violin—for the reason that there was, I
had been informed, a flaw in the tone of its upper reg-
ister.

We had moved into the "Agassiz" apartment house at
191 Commonwealth Avenue after the end of the war,
and there my youngest daughter, Jean, was born. She
was the first child in many decades to enter the world
within this substantial but old-fashioned building, a
building which belonged to Major Henry Lee Higginson and had been erected when he was young to house
his growing family and those of his friends, the selfsame
Major Higginson who founded the Symphony Orchestra forty years earlier. He had become a hero to me on
that account and it pleased me to know that the same
roof now sheltered us both. I had been recently told that

another hero of mine, Henry Adams, had considered coming here to live, that shortly after his marriage he had written Major Higginson from Paris to ask whether the new building might be a proper dwelling for his bride and himself.

Built of red brick in the 1870s, it was six stories high and it occupied many feet on the Avenue and around the corner along Exeter Street. The entrance hall held a dado of blue and white tiles below ocher-colored walls, and the trim was of varnished wood. From here mounted an immense metal staircase, blatantly fire-proof, which I never saw put to use save as a shelter, beneath its wide structure on the ground floor, for Jean's baby carriage. The front elevator, however, be-came a real part of our lives, carrying us and its resigned attendant at a leisurely pace beyond the two lower stories to the austere hallway of our own third floor, where the skylight from above insistently illuminated the crude look of metal and wood. Now and then we had to await the ascent during many long moments, ringing in vain for the sound of the pulley rope as the elevator moved between floors. All was silence save for muffled human voices far above. Then, finally, when the door opened at ground level, an old gentleman came forth, cane in hand, attired for the outdoors, a courteous old gentleman who bowed his greeting as the elevator at-tendant went to open the street door.

"Sorry to keep you waiting, Ma'am," the attendant said as he took me upward. "Colonel Pierson needed help with his rubbers. He didn't care to chance the rain today with all them clouds in the sky."

Once we were inside our door, the aspect changed.

Here were walls of gray and gold, curtains the color of sunshine at the tall windows, and a glow that suffused the aspect of the rooms, high of stud, along the sunny stretch of Commonwealth Avenue. Little save the initial structural form had been present when we took over the flat from charter members of the original Agassiz group in this the first apartment house of Boston. Our predecessors had managed successfully to resist newfangled ideas and it had amazed me to see what could be done in the way of opposing the march of progress. Rooms trimmed with fumed oak had been carefully sheltered from sunshine by day, and at evening the light falling from small bulbs attached to the transformed, bent-elbowed gas brackets of an earlier era was scarcely brighter. In the dining room a pair of carved teakwood corner-cupboard screens imitated an openwork Arab design, and it was fascinating to see the pattern of dust left on my finger as I inserted then withdrew it from one of the openings. The kitchen, pantries and bathrooms were ample in space but somber with the tin and soap-stone linings of former days. These, with our advent, were changed to white porcelain. I remember how startled we were on the afternoon of our first entry when we saw an elderly, white-haired man open the front door without a signal of any kind and walk deliberately from one room to another. It was Major Higginson himself, come from his own apartment above to investigate the decorative doings of young moderns such as we. He lingered for many minutes in the newly white-tiled master's bathroom, seating himself opposite it to stare at the gleaming bathtub on clawed feet, a six-foot tub recently installed.

Beneath our roof the four blue-eyed blonds, in addition to the governess and the nursemaid who kept their rooms and clothes in order, became almost an army corps, especially when playmates dropped in for a visit. Yet, down the Exeter Street hallway, army headquarters, the rooms contained each a separate existence. The room at the far end, largest and most substantially furnished, belonged to Elizabeth, known as Betsy. Here she worked each afternoon over her school assignments, in particular the mathematics upon which her teacher laid much stress. Going down the hall late one day, I found her at her desk, pencil in hand, mouth firmly set, eyes full of determination.

"I've absolutely got to solve this arithmetic problem even if I don't believe I ever can," she said, and looked up at me. "It's just exactly like trying to push through the middle of a stone wall with your bare hands, don't you think? But it makes you feel strong when you've done it. I like that feeling."

"Yes, dear," I agreed. "Hold on to that feeling. It can help you in all sorts of ways."

Walking back toward the living room, absorbed for the moment in this child's outlook and character, I remembered the day when the first labor pains struck with astonishing ferocity to announce her coming, a coming which, in spite of determination, hers and mine, took almost eighteen long hours that seemed to be without end. And I remembered how prolonged was my lassitude after her arrival, when I lay for more than a week in the great, old-fashioned family bed placed close to the window in my room at Beverly overlooking the sea. I had not realized in those early days, perhaps because of my youth and my ignorance of the suffering in the world, how blessed I was in all that I could call my own: the devotion of a grateful husband who looked with love upon the charms of our new baby, and my surroundings of more than ordinary "comfort and joy," as the carol sings it. I wanted only to be alone to read Mrs. Gaskell or the simple, heart-warming tales of William De Morgan about the lives of unworldly people, or else to stare into the fire that burned on the hearth, to gaze at the flowers in their vases above the mantel, to watch rose petals open in the soft silence all about and to wonder about the beginning of life and its ending. Every few hours a voluminous, competent woman in starched uniform and cap, specialist in the care of the newborn, full-bosomed, cheerful, her path assured as that of a prairie schooner, entered the room carrying my babe in her wide arms, a quiet babe already wise who began at once when placed close to me, as if instructed by some nameless power, to nurse at my breast. And now here she was, my first-born, in her early teens: capable, sure, sensitive, a young woman in embryo who had once been a part of the confusions and difficult adaptations of early marriage when her father and her mother had known one another barely longer than the nine months allotted to gestation. Yet she stood on firm ground, forever fixed as the symbol of that first union. She possessed the quality of a figurehead riding the waves before a ship in full sail, gallant, indestructible. Only her mother knew of the swift fears that had laid their hand on her as a little girl, fear of storms and the wild wind blowing, fear of the dreams darkly coloring the long spaces of night.

Priscilla came next, a Puritan maid destined to cling to her Boston beginnings, child of equanimity and impulse in equal degree, warm of heart, vigorous, straightforward, undemanding, easily moved to laughter. During the months before her birth at summer's end, I had lived at the pace of a Roman charioteer. I had driven my car back and forth up and down the long shore road that wound between our house and the fishing port of Gloucester, and, seated in a speeding motorboat, I had crossed and recrossed the waters of Marblehead Bay where my husband raced his three-meter boat, Marconi-rigged, swift as light, against those of the Germans who had come from Kiel: lively days lacking the overtones of doubt, days without complexity. It seemed as if Priscilla must have been infected by this genial, healthy existence. For the rigors of life fell without complexity on her youthful mind so that her sanguine appearance continued to match her sanguine spirit.

Alongside the nursery was the narrow room belonging to our son John, named for his father and known as Jock. Born on an April day, the aftermath of storm on a hilltop in the Beverly house above the sea, his arrival followed a wait of many weeks, weeks of protracted solitude while my husband campaigned at large for a seat in Congress. Jock, whose birth was swift as the wait was long, brought joy to the house of his ancestors, to his father, to me.

"You have a fine boy," said the doctor.

"He will be Chief Justice of the Supreme Court," I murmured, and closed my eyes to drift into sleep.

Now at the age of nine he had already become a personage, intent upon his thoughts, upon the words set down in books, even as I had been intent on these things during the months before his advent.

Dwelling one day on the laws that govern inheritance, as I talked with a friend who had borne more than the usual number of offspring, I described my own experience.

"Each of my children appears to have followed the pattern set up by me while I was carrying them," I said.

"It's the other way around," she answered with an authority based on long experience. "The child you are carrying determines your own behavior at the time. You don't become a free agent until it has seen the light of day." The idea was seemingly logical and also pleasant. For it presupposed inherent strength in the coming generation. I hoped it might be true.

Jock's qualities seemed to be those on which to build a bright future. He was reticent and sure, quick to perceive inner meaning, gentle, brave. It was his habit to spend long hours by himself while he read, stretched out on his bed after school, occupied, when still young for this sort of fare, with Kingsley's *Water Babies* and *Westward Ho!* or Jules Verne's *Twenty Thousand Leagues Under the Sea.* Indeed, his love of books was such that often he read late into the night, turning on the bedside light after I had put it out as I tucked him in. When morning came, sleepy as he was, it was not easy to pry him from bed, and frequently he was late for breakfast, thereby keeping the Chestnut Hill school bus waiting at the door below. Finally we laid down an ultimatum, his father and I: the bus could not be asked to wait for Jock, a single individual. Further tardiness would mean that he must find his own way to school.

"I don't mind," the boy answered. "I'd like to go to Chestnut Hill alone. You treat me too much as if I'm still a baby." Challenge to a jousting match.

On the morning that the new policy was put to proof, when he was barely eight years old, I watched uneasily from the dining room window until he had achieved the crowded crossing at Commonwealth Avenue, watched him as far as I could see while he walked, a small, resolute figure, toward Huntington Avenue and the trolley car that would carry him to Chestnut Hill. Then I went to the telephone begging the school secretary to let me know when Jock had arrived. Of how many painful moments does the process of growth consist.

Another, and the last, of my children was Jean with her innocent air that called forth a protective gesture from any who were near. I remembered an Atlantic crossing when she was still a baby on our way to the coast of Normandy. The Captain of the liner in gallant French fashion invited her to his top bridge where she could have the full benefit of sun and air, where she could become "a flower of the sea," he said. Here, day after quiet day, she lay in her basket close below his lookout, a sleeping beauty and mermaid combined. Jean's present manner of gaiety, her iridescence, like a rainbow arching the sky, was a part of her tenderness and her charm, serving as an unconscious defense against a potentially tragic world.

On weekends during the school term and during all the summer months, we left Commonwealth Avenue, driving to Topsfield, our country place on the Ipswich River, where we had gone to live on quitting the house at Beverly. We drove in a wide, accommodating Pierce Arrow with our chauffeur, William Lavoie, at the wheel. He was a small, agile French Canadian and for many years remained with us as dependable guide and friend. We drove the same route always, out of Boston, past the Massachusetts General Hospital on the lower esplanade and past the prison in Charlestown, where at a certain moment in time I was to see armed guards pacing the high outer ramp on duty to prevent the escape of Sacco and Vanzetti and to bar entrance for their sympathizers. I remember turning quickly away from this sight, which brought nothing but horror to the imagination. We continued, then, along the Newburyport Turnpike to a junction leading downward toward the Ipswich River valley, thence to River Road, our road, where we turned into an avenue flanked by handsome Carolina hemlocks planted at the instance of Professor Sargent.

The house on its maple-ringed knoll seemed always to promise peace, standing over the river, its grassy terraces bounded by low stone walls. A passage on the east led to the children's wing. It was here that I went to watch the young play the charades they delighted in acting out for their elders or to listen as the three older ones waved their arms in rhythm with the music, singing:

> I saw three ships go sailing by
> On Christmas day in the morning . . .

It was here that I read aloud to them each evening from "John Gilpin," from *Black Beauty* or the *Tanglewood Tales,* and later, in their bedrooms, tucked them in for the night. On the west, beyond a miniature greenhouse, a pair of steps dropped to the music room, replica of one in a Florentine palace. A kind of magic touched this room between the soaring vaults of the ceiling and the floor beneath, a floor of large alternating walnut and teakwood squares in lengthy progression toward the tall windows at the south. The magic pursued him who stepped through the open windows of summer upon a terrace to sit on grass or stone wall listening to the music and dreaming by the slow light of the moon.

The room at the right of the front door, my husband's den, belonged in particular to him, a pine-paneled room with glass-encased racks holding his fine collection of guns, their stocks brightly polished. There at an immense mahogany desk he conducted the business of our acres and the various houses scattered about them. One of these on River Road had once been the local schoolhouse and still carried the belfry and the bell which during the long years had rung to summon the young across the fields.

My own part in the life at Topsfield was various and variable, with many choices spread before me: the terrace garden where I went to work in flower beds or to read above the river when household planning was at an end and guests had gone their way; playing my violin with some friend at the piano; making waffles for the children at luncheon in the bow window of the dining room, four after another four, on the electric waffle iron; talking the long evening through with some poet or philosopher who had come to stay in the house. Anything seemed possible to me, any bright and gleaming thing, any form of creation, any effort of good will.

My failures, my frustrations, were chiefly centered in golf and bridge, fashionable among our friends, both of these pursuits set in and about the Myopia Club nearby. Here, on weekends in summer, there were golf tournaments known as Tombstone Tournaments wherein partners, male and female, were chosen by lot. In spite of the series of lessons given me, I had not been able to learn golf properly and had been consistently worsted by everyone with whom I played excepting one young woman who, being nearsighted, held a *lorgnon* with one hand and swung her club with the other. One tournament in particular, in which the word tombstone was essentially significant, brought me so much shame, so great a sense of defeat, that later I abandoned golf forever. I had drawn, in apparent good luck, a top player, an arrogant young man very sure of his own superiority. After lunch, when the entire party was gathered at the tenth hole, it fell to me to drive off first. On ahead was a water hazard some thirty feet in extent and, terrified as I was, with all eyes watching, I drove my ball straight into the water, thereby not only losing the ball but being fined several points as well. My attempts at bridge were hardly more fortunate. At Myopia the players were excellent and the stakes high. Once I was asked to make a fourth at a table of devotees, great specialists in the game. At a bid by my partner of five no trumps doubled from which I had to extricate us—with a large sum of money hanging on the outcome—I happened to glance down on a yellow rose pinned to my dress over my left breast. It responded wildly to the beating of my heart as in mortal fear I played my cards.

In Boston we continued to a certain extent, my husband and I, with the formal dinners become familiar to us when we were bride and groom. I had learned to

enjoy these dinners as, gradually, I became intimate
with the people who were my husband's old friends. Several men, in particular, I enjoyed as partners at the dinner
table. One of these was Dr. Harvey Cushing, the brain
surgeon. Small, slim, with alert black eyes, he was aware
of as many aspects of our world as though all of time
were his to dispose of. And yet, I realized, watching
his swift gesture and eager manner, he had yet another
sort of vast and concentrated energy to give to the work
which had brought him fame.

"But, Dr. Cushing," I said impulsively one evening as
dessert was being served us, "aren't you terribly alarmed,
doesn't your heart set up a tremendous pounding, when
you have a human skull open on the operating table below your surgeon's scalpel? Isn't it almost more than
you can bear? To be that sort of god looking on from
above?"

"Yes, my dear lady, it *is* almost more than I can bear
—continually so," he answered, and for a moment was
silent.

Another dinner party friend was Mr. William Endicott,
known as Black Bill because of his heavy black beard.
He and his charming wife were intimates of Professor
Sargent, and both were assiduous gardeners. On the
grounds of their country place at Danvers there was, in
addition to many fine and unusual trees, a narrowly
mounting circular edifice known as a gazebo. Built in
the early nineteenth century, when leisure for the well-
to-do was plentiful and manners were a delight, this
building became, now and then, a refuge for my husband and me when we were invited to drink tea on the

gazebo balcony from where we could see the beauties of the flowering shrubs and the roses in bloom below. I felt myself a participant in The Thousand and One Nights as I sipped my China tea from a delicate Canton cup in this exotic setting.

The advent into our household of John Singer Sargent was a great pleasure. My friendship with the painter began when I made a professional visit to his studio in the Fenway that he might draw a portrait of me in charcoal. Although the necessity rather bored him, he had engaged himself since his return to Boston during the latter years of his life in making these likenesses in black-and-white. Several friends of ours were sitting for him just then, but my drawing, when finished, varied from the others because of the care and time he had given to the accurate rendering of a Spanish shawl I had inadvertently wrapped about myself on the cold day of my first sitting. Mr. Sargent had been attracted by its color and design, pale yellow flowers on a background of dark brown, and had eagerly transferred its image onto paper. The extra hours I thus spent with him, going to the studio twice or thrice rather than once, as was usual, made for prolonged conversation and for friendship. He told me anecdotes of his life and the lives of certain among his friends. He talked to me of Alice Meynell, the poet, an intimate of his, describing the details of her often lacerating life, surrounded as she was by artists and writers for whom defeat and despair and disease were the order of the day, telling me also of her continually assuaging gesture toward them all, toward Francis Thompson especially. I had long ago made up my mind, on reading her two lovely poems in *The Oxford Book of English Verse*, that she was one of the gifted creatures of the earth:

> She holds her little thoughts in sight,
>   Though gay they run and leap.
> She is so circumspect and right
>   She has her soul to keep . . .

These lines from "the Lady of the Lambs" described, I was certain, their author herself, and the image I had of her was enhanced by John Sargent's story.

Concerning Mr. Sargent's own life, he had had enough, he said, of his fashionable oil portraits of the rich, and his interest was centered at present on the techniques required for the painting of murals. Those in the Boston Public Library having been completed at an earlier day, he was now in process of discovering a method for the murals which were to decorate the Fine Arts Museum. Meanwhile, an amateur pianist, it pleased him to keep his fingers flexible and sure in order to play the accompaniments to the French songs he so greatly admired, those of Fauré in particular. "Pure line, pure line," he said, describing the music of this composer, making a gesture of illustration with his stick of charcoal. His difficulty, he continued, was that of impressing a singer into service. The professionals were too much occupied and obliged, also, to save their voices for practice and for public performance, while the amateurs were musically unreliable, taking liberties with the composer's scheme.

"Best to hum the melody myself, I find. Fewer outrages committed that way," he said.

"I wonder," I asked, "how the Fauré songs would sound with the melody played on the violin."

Mr. Sargent paused, charcoal stick held motionless. "I should think very well," he answered with a note of the tentative in his voice.

"I've several times played *Les Roses d'Ispahan* and *Après un Rève,*" I said. "How lovely they are!"

"And what of *Les Berceaux?* Have you tried that on your fiddle?"

"No, but I'd like to. The melody is slow and simple."

It ended in my inviting him to tea, in my taking the fiddle from its box, in our playing Fauré and Duparc and Reynaldo Hahn as the minutes fled toward evening. John Singer Sargent, painter, was cousin to Charles Sprague Sargent, arboriculturist, and they resembled each other in the urgency of their enthusiasm, their application to the muse who directed each. I had once again become a tool to the undeviating purpose of an elderly man whose genius held him chained to youth.

Several among us during these years, those who had a love for chamber music and wished to become more familiar with its literature, decided on engaging a professional string quartet to play for us at regular intervals. We incorporated ourselves as a Chamber Music Club, took in members on a sliding scale of dues, the rich contributing more for the privilege of belonging, the poor less, and, among house rules during recitals, smoking was to be allowed and lights dimmed. The men who played to us once a month were the principals of their sections in the Boston Symphony who thus, for the first time, formed an organization among themselves. It was understood that three members of the governing committee were to select the music for each concert, one classic quartet, one modern. Edward Pickman, the historian, and I were entrusted with the choice of the first, and young Theodore Chanler, beginning then to write his own compositions, chose the quartet of contemporary date.

We looked forward in immense anticipation to these evenings and with reason, the musicians gaining in skill as they worked together, the audience becoming a more and more lively part. Bejeweled dowagers and attendant husbands came on from dinner parties, students in their tweeds left Cambridge by subway or trolley to follow the music, score in hand, while we of the committee felt ourselves the present day counterpart of the Margrave of Brandenburg, patron of Bach. The meetings at the outset were held in various private houses, but soon a larger space became desirable, one which should be constant. We engaged a floor in a building on Newbury Street near Arlington, then headquarters for the Academy of Arts and Sciences and once the town house of Alexander Agassiz. I liked to imagine that the ghost of the lively patron of the arts hovered about us, mingling, perhaps more completely than we mortals could do, with the overtones of the music.

These many amenities and pleasures, alternating with the arduous toil of common day, embroidered my life during the years in Boston, years which unspun as a roll of straw matting from the far port of Hong Kong. Indeed, life in New England was still haunted by that Far Eastern influence which, like salt spray along the masts of schooners, had permeated the background surrounding the families of those bold Salem traders whose

East Indiamen, sails spread wide, drove homeward in ninety-five days from Calcutta, outward in ninety-two days to Canton, whose distant ports of entry—Mozambique, Zanzibar, Aden, Sumatra, Muscat—beckoned like a tale from *The Arabian Nights*.

My husband's puritanical upbringing at the hands of a spinster aunt, born in Salem, who thriftily purchased woolen stuff by the bolt from which to cut suits for the boys and jumpers for the girls, was nonetheless tempered by the presence of relics from that mythical time when summer brought forth dresses of white muslin, jackets of Madras linen, broad-brimmed hats from Panama and palm-leaf fans, along with the smell of lilacs. From childhood he had taken for granted cornice moldings in gold leaf, fine porcelain, chairs of teakwood, sewing tables of gilt-inlaid papier-mâché, ornaments of ivory, elephant tusks, carved Buddhas from Java, Chinese fire screens, ormolu girandoles with lusters that tinkled in the breeze, camphor, dates, ginger in green Canton jars, cheroots, and the rockets and sparklers that streaked the night sky to drift downward in slow rhythm like the falling waters of fountains at the end of day.

If for me, interloper from a less romantic land, this background could never become a complete unit of my being, never entirely contain me, I felt it in its pervading charm. And so I could disclose its nature to my children, of whose inheritance it was rightfully a part.

Boston, "the hub of the solar system" for Oliver Wendell Holmes, the substance, for me, of family and friendship, of labor and love.

14

PARIS FINALE

In a month of May, during the 1920s, I sailed on the S.S. *Île de France* bound for Le Havre, full of plans for buying antique French furniture and a few paintings to ornament our country house at Topsfield. It had not been absolutely necessary to go abroad to buy furnishings for the house, but our architect thought well of it and my husband had given his consent, even his blessing, in order that my long-lived love for France might be indulged once again. I had made quantities of trips to France since the early years of my life, but the idea of setting forth afresh for those friendly shores, where the natives were less like strangers than kin, invariably brought an accelerated beat to my heart. It seemed as though destiny pointed its unerring finger in that direction.

The crossing itself was pleasant as always on French ships, but not memorable: long hours of sleep to break the rhythm brought by exertion at home, haphazard conversation with fellow passengers, days spent in a deck chair wrapped in sun or soft mists, reading without interruption from telephone, from questions requiring answers, from decisions demanding action. Among my books was Louis Bromfield's *The Strange Case of Miss Annie Spragg,* sent me by the author as a sailing-away present.

The Bromfields, Louis and Mary, had been much at our house during the moments when they were not in the West or in France, and a part of his first successful book, *The Green Bay Tree,* was written at Topsfield. On fair mornings during that summer when the wind blew from the west, I could hear the tap-tap of his typewriter mingling with the note of the red-winged blackbird, the sounds joining waves of heat that shimmered along the meadow grass between the house and the Ipswich River below, where, in a spot of shade, Bromfield had gone to write. When evening came he rested from the labors of creation, stretched full length on a sofa or on the floor of our expansive music room, listening to the piano, voice or violin. Later, the music at an end, he pulled himself up to smoke, to drink, to talk on and on, halfway toward the light of morning.

The book, *Annie Spragg,* was, at the moment of my sailing, a tremendous best seller, and one afternoon as I put it down on my deck chair to walk the daily mile, a stranger stood beside me, a large, full-bosomed young woman with mascara-ringed eyes and heavy wind-driven hair. I had, during the days past, become accustomed to seeing her tour the deck or sit in the bar with a hapless, watery-eyed youth of fragile physique.

"Pardon me," she said, "I've been watching while you read this *Annie Spragg* book. I see now you've gone most of the way through and so I ask would you possibly let me have it for a day or two when you're done."

"Why, yes," I said as she went on to explain.

"Not that I get much time for reading, but that book seems such a sensation right now I thought I'd like to carry it round for a while so folks could get a look at it in my hands."

We presently landed, and on the first evening ashore I was taken by a friend to call on the Gerald Murphys, who lived in a seventeenth-century building on the quai des Grands Augustins, that most ancient part of Paris. Climbing the several flights of unlighted, antique stairs to gain the Murphy flat above, each tread hand-hewed from an unyielding block of wood, the angles and turns awkward to negotiate in the dark, I had arrived, with a shock, in Elysium. I entered a room that hung high above the river, an unassuming square, its walls of white plaster unevenly applied in the manner of the early craftsman. But here the ancient and hoary came abruptly to an end, for the recessed windows were hung with curtains of vermilion taffeta fresh and brilliant and crisp as newly cut, high-growing flowers. The grand piano above a floor of polished black held for decoration a set of ball bearings in a circular metal frame, and opposite, a stand with delicate metal legs and black formica top was spread with crystal vases loaded with the flowering branches of spring. White violets in a low bowl rested on a coffee table beside the crimson-covered sofa, and on the chimney breast above the live embers of a fire hung a recent likeness of Charlie Chaplin in wood, limp arms and baggy trousers abstractly carved by the Murphys' great friend Fernand Léger, the cubist painter.

Several people were there as I came in, but it was Léger

who especially took me in charge, who guided me to an open casement from where we looked down upon the moon-struck surfaces and the deeply gathered shadows about Notre Dame across the Seine.

"*C'est bien beau, est vrai, Madame?*"

It was indeed beautiful enough to have been a portion of paradise. We could not at that hour watch a part of the traditional Paris scene, familiar to me from other years and belonging to the lower rather than to the upper regions of our sphere, a scene enacted by the *pêcheurs* and the *remorqueurs,* for these representatives of proletarian Paris rested briefly from their labors as they waited for dawn and the wan streak of light athwart the sky which once more set them in motion, the former with rods baited for fish at the side of the river, the latter with rods hooked for the dusty gathering of rags and papers.

I was at once drawn to Sara and Gerald Murphy, into the current that flowed about them, drawn willingly as though for good and all. This was an instance of the spell they cast, the sense of permanence they gave to the atmosphere about them. For they possessed a genius for friendship and the ability to create a setting in which friendship continued to grow. Presently, they were to become allies of Scott Fitzgerald, who in his novel *Tender Is the Night* is believed by some to have chosen the Murphys as models for Dick and Nicole Diver when, at the outset of the book, this pair were united at their happiest and best. Indeed, various passages touching upon the Divers' first felicitous years and their colony of attendant friends appear as unmistakable character sketches of Gerald and Sara Murphy.

They had been at table half an hour and a percepti-
ble change had set in—person by person had given
up something, a preoccupation, an anxiety, a sus-
picion, and now they were only their best selves
and the Divers' guests . . . the two Divers began
suddenly to warm and glow and expand . . . they
seemed to speak to every one at the table, singly and
together, assuring them of their friendliness, their
affection. And for a moment the faces turned up toward them were like the faces of poor children at a
Christmas tree.

The consensus among the company gathered at the
Murphy flat that evening was that I should give up any
idea of purchasing furniture out of an earlier epoch.

"Why not live in your own time?" Sara asked in the
downright yet kindly manner with which she might
have corrected her own children.

"Possibly plans have already gone too far to allow for
change," Gerald said, always tactful and conciliatory.

"Sapristi! On fait du moins ce qu'on veut," Léger in-
terjected, unable to make a decisive point in any but his
own tongue.

I remained silent, thoughtful, as I envisaged, and later
brought about, one of the compromises necessary when
the line of action cannot be redrawn according to some
pleasantly fresh but tardily calculated scheme. Before I
left home my husband and I had agreed that the extra
furniture chosen for the house should be antique French:
armchairs for the drawing room and a table or two for
my bedroom where a mantel of Verona marble and a
dark wood floor seemed to call for walnut. And, my hus-

band said, that if I decided to ornament the dining room walls with one or more paintings, a pastoral scene might fit in best.

As things turned out, I went back to Massachusetts having bought a gracefully modern set of gilt dining room chairs, suitable anywhere, a pair of antique *fauteuils,* three of Léger's abstract water colors for my bedroom and also an oil of Jacques Émile Blanche, a man belonging to an older generation, whose work was direct and readily understood.

This picture was named the "Heritage of the Admiral" and was based on a passage from a book called *Le Potomak* by Jean Cocteau, just then at the height of his fame. With a sea scene and sailing ship as background, a table in the foreground covered with Chinese embroidery held a shell frame, mother-of-pearl opera glasses, china dish, gaudy satin-lined box and other objects usually associated with the days of Salem shipping. It seemed a fitting ornament to our house, whose quality belonged in great measure to the Salem tradition.

Before leaving the Murphys' flat on that first evening, Fernand Léger suggested taking me on the following afternoon to the Grand Palais to see the annual picture exhibition at the Salle des Indépendents. I accepted with a pleasure tempered somewhat by doubts of my ability to digest the work of the modern painters.

We stood side by side under a warm sun, after finishing the rounds of the exhibit, pausing at the head of the steps leading downward from the Grand Palais. The grass along the borders of the Champs Élysées was green and without blemish, the horse chestnuts had opened their leaves in classic perfection, and among the leaves white flower spikes pointed toward heaven like those white candles placed by the true believer before the altar of his Lady. To right and to left bright tulips in circular beds were being watered by attentive gardeners just as, long ago, when I was a child in a gingham dress on a spring day, gardeners watered the flower beds in Gramercy Park. Standing beside Léger, I knew that these manifestations of spring were everywhere and yet I could not see them in the fullness of their splendor because my eyes were blinded by the colors I had left behind inside the Palais.

"Monsieur Léger," I asked, "how can you admire pictures that take away the beauty of sun and sky and grass and flowers, pictures that give the lie to nature?" I waved an arm over what lay below—what, at present, seemed merely drab. I waited eagerly for his answer, something that might convince not alone me but also my husband and our friends at home. This last, I reflected, might be more difficult. After all, it was I who had gone forth to investigate, I who had been already caught up in the excitement of the new. How expect those others, more steadfast than I, to be infected with a contagion so recent as mine? I sighed in perplexity and turned toward Monsieur Léger, awaiting his answer.

"You must remember, Madame," he said, "that the Impressionists, with Monet as leader, went so far in their imitation of nature, representing each mere quiver of wind, each ray of light, to such a degree of the authentic, that to proceed further along that path was impossible."

I looked at my new friend, sincere and earnest artist

that he was, in amusement as well as admiration. There was in his pronunciation of the word *"impossible,"* spoken in French, the final *i* drawn out at great length, a definite closing of the door upon the past. This was the start of my indoctrination.

On another afternoon, when Léger invited me to the galleries of Léonce Rosenberg, the dealer, where many of his own canvases were on display, I took a real step in emancipation. We stood for long moments before one particular picture, a picture representing the cubed symbols of some reality too complex to be grasped by the uninstructed layman. He attempted then to inform, to arouse in me an understanding of idea, of method.

"Here," he said, "you see the effort of five, six, seven years, an effort prodigious, even terrible, in the energy demanded of him who struggled, a veritable wrestling match."

Glancing at this man, solid and foursquare and honest, I saw his straightforward eyes of a Norman peasant fixed upon the canvas, his lips compressed in reminiscence, his forehead creased.

"A struggle?" I asked.

"But certainly. Was I not obliged to find my way like each of us who desires to move forward, desires not merely to repeat himself? This picture with its base of cubism became my five-finger exercises as also it announced my creed."

I gazed on it with the concentration demanded of me, while gradually new understanding seemed to break through the stubborn spaces of my mind.

Following the passage of years, when recently I spent

a summer in Europe, I realized once again how little one can foresee of what the future may bring in the way of judgment to works of art. At the Tate Gallery in London that summer, coming on an exhibition of John Sargent's oil portraits, great magnificent creations, I was told by the museum guard that a room dedicated to the painter was permanently to house these masterpieces. Here were the canvases representing that section of Sargent's work toward which he had been least compelled, which at the latter part of his life he had almost repudiated. Again, during that same trip, reaching Holland and driving out to the forest of Otterloo to see the famous Kroller-Müller collection of painting and sculpture, I had been confronted in surprise by Léger's first cubist picture, the one which we had studied together when I was young. Hanging among others, this early example, modest in tone, quietly unobtrusive, spoke to me of the past and reminded me that with this very canvas as stepping-stone, the painter had made his name secure in the history of French art. As I left the gallery I blew it a kiss, and any who saw might well have been puzzled. For, by comparison with the work of his mature years, it appeared innocuous indeed.

I remembered then the words of Gertrude Stein, that strange woman who, as a child, had with her brother evolved a private language which their elders could not follow and who left behind at her death books heralded by a few but little understood by the mass of men. In one small work of hers, *Composition as Explanation,* I had come on phrases written in her consciously childlike manner that expressed her ideas on the evolution of art and human resistance to change.

> The creator of the new composition in the arts is
> an outlaw until he is a classic, there is hardly a mo-
> ment in between and it is really too bad very much
> too bad naturally for the creator but also very much
> too bad for the enjoyer, they all really would enjoy
> the created so much better just after it has been made
> than when it is already a classic. . . .

How true, and yet how impossible for the "enjoyer" to
mend his ways. And I thought not only of the artists and
musicians of the present moment but of those who had
lived unappreciated, unhappy, in other eras.

A year or so after my solitary trip to Paris in quest of
furnishings for our house at home, we arrived as a family
to occupy a house on the rue de l'Élysée overlooking the
palace which was the residence of the French President.
Our children ranged from three to thirteen, and for all
of us it was a fascinating game to stand on the balcony
that opened from an upper-story window and watch the
retinue of visiting royalty as it drove through the palace
grounds, gates flung wide for grand occasions such as
these. Rather less agreeable, but more continuous, was
the presence of the guard who acted as armed sentinel on
duty before his sentry house at the gate. An unending
partisan of the law he seemed to us, who could not forget
the fate of the luckless Guignol, and we were ever anx-
ious to escape his stern and searching eye.

Our taking possession of the house as a band had not
been without confusion. My husband was detained for a
time in Boston and the details were left to me. We descended upon it, empty for several years and freshly re-
furnished and decorated, like a flock of starlings on a

newly sown meadow. Once inside, we made haste to establish ourselves and, as an aid to unpacking when evening fell, lighted each room and bath so that from without, the house must have outrivaled in brilliance the President's palace across the way. Suddenly, much in the pattern of those afflicted ones in early Bible history, we were surrounded by darkness, all things coming to a halt. This was followed by a pounding on the front door, which Paul, our agile and enterprising butler, answered, candle in hand. From the street came a sound of American voices, American laughter. Here were a pair of friends and neighbors arrived with a bouquet of roses to welcome our establishment. They had rung the doorbell but its sound had gone dead along with the lights. We had probably blown out the main fuse, they told us, from turning on too much electric power at one moment.

"Only spoiled foreigners like yourselves would consider such an illumination necessary," they said.

"You mean that we can light only one or two rooms at a time?" I asked.

"Perhaps three or four at a time. What's the difference? Why be in such an infernal hurry? Remember the way they do things over here." And the two went off to report our dilemma to the company concerned, leaving me with the roses in my arms, quantities of stiff-stemmed, sweet-smelling white buds. There were always compensations, I told myself.

Another cause for confusion requiring instant remedy was the lack of everyday commonplace objects essential to a caravansary such as ours. The decorator in charge of furnishing had had an eye for style and elegance, placing inlaid cabinets and a magnificent Aubusson carpet along the floor of the salon but neglecting to consider the needs of small children, space for storing clothes, cupboards for toys. In the kitchen our broad-faced, capable cook, who looked like the mother of Louise in Charpentier's opera, was helpless, she said, because of the limited number of copper pots provided, the lack of strainers for hot milk and chocolate, the absence of *bains-maries*. After a time, these various items were supplied and we settled to the everyday routine.

The older children attended *Cours,* classes which, in approved French custom, required the assistance of an afternoon visiting governess come to drill the young people in their work for the following day: memorizing dates of history, lines of prose, lines of poetry, to be recited in class. I was gratified as the weeks went past to be told by the directress of the Cours that my children did surprisingly well when one remembered that they were, after all, Americans. They brought, nonetheless, many a heartache and annoyance to their Mademoiselle in failing to memorize passages with the docility to which she was accustomed, insisting, rather, on discovering what and when and why.

"A t'on jamais vu des enfants pareils?" she asked, and I found it difficult to reply. *"Ils ne font que demander des questions!"*

For me the mechanics of life should include music, and the making of music required a piano in addition to the violin which awaited the proper moment for removal from its case. And so I went, presently, to the office of the Pleyel company in order to rent one of their grand pianos. They regretted, the answer was, that their large pianos were all engaged. Could I possibly make use of a piano with double keyboard? Of these there were but four in existence. One was available should I decide to consider it. A splendid instrument, they assured me. The piano was shown me, rather longer than its single counterpart and lacking the broad curve on the treble side, an oblong with keyboard at each end, the two sets of strings running crisscross beneath the hammers. A person wishing to use it alone could, by pushing a lever, cut off the vibration of one set of the strings, pulling it out when two persons desired to play simultaneously. This seemed an ingenious arrangement, the instrument was a majestic structure of gleaming black, and in our high-ceilinged salon there was room for it against a wall opposite the fireplace. Best of all, it might magnetize, like a lowering beast with hypnotic eye, the musicians necessary to its constitution, musicians otherwise difficult for a stranger like myself to come upon.

The fame of the double Pleyel, indeed, spread so fast and so far that not only my friends and the local pianists but strangers from a distance begged to be allowed to use it. One morning a professional woman pianist came to practice the Beethoven Concerto No. 4 in G Major at her end of the instrument, while at the other a coach played the orchestral score. She was preparing herself for a concert in Amsterdam under Mengelberg. Another pair, father and daughter, arrived from the suburbs, coming for their own—but chiefly, I believe, for the father's— pleasure. The daughter, stoop-shouldered from assiduous practice at the keyboard, had memorized the waltzes of Chopin, which she rendered methodically obedient to the metronome. The father, meanwhile, facing her, embroidered arabesques of his own contriving about her

earnestly regular rhythms, his fingers engaging the keys
in an ecstasy of wandering sound as he strove to outdo
the Polish composer on their common ground. There
were also the adherents of modern music who came to
play the scores of Stravinsky, in particular that of *Oedi-
pus Rex,* which the composer had himself arranged for
two pianos. A wonderfully passionate and solemn dissonance took its way through the house on the day we
first listened to this magnum opus, a day when March
gales in apparent sympathy wildly shook the building
from without.

One evening in our salon, perhaps the most complete
among others in the pleasure it gave, brought the French
singer, Madame Croisa, of partly Greek blood, to bestow
her talents upon us. She had become a friend when my
husband took me to Brussels to visit his classmate at
Harvard, William Phillips, and his wife, then Ambassador and Ambassadress to Belgium. Aware of my love
for music, they had invited us to stay on the occasion of
Croisa's midwinter recital at the Embassy.

We had arrived at Brussels by train and were met on
the platform by the Ambassador and an undersecretary,
both very smart and correct in appearance. We, too, had
done our best in the matter of clothes, my husband upright and handsome in his derby hat and well-cut, velvet-
collared overcoat; I in fur jacket and muff, and a toque
of matching fur of which I was enamored because it
resembled one I had seen in a painting by Manet. Just
after descending the train steps and shaking hands with
our host, a most agreeable occasion which I had for
several weeks anticipated with pleasure, my panties—the
small pearl button fastening them become suddenly un-

sewn—fell to the platform. This was an occurrence which could not be dissembled. There they lay, a mass of inert white fluff, as fellow passengers walked past and the Ambassador stood above, caught in a situation with which he had never before been obliged to deal. Swiftly, my cheeks pink with shame, I stooped to gather them up before the young secretary should attempt to do so and slipped them inside my muff. We walked on, a dignified foursome, but I felt the irretrievable disgrace that a child knows when caught by the grownups in a trap not of his own contriving.

Events as they followed at the Embassy brought relief from humiliation, brought forgetfulness of everything save the quite wonderful moments that unrolled like a scene in an absorbing play wherein, miraculously, I had found myself to be a part. The recital took place in the Embassy ballroom, and fifty or sixty people had gathered to occupy the gilt chairs which of themselves in any house, any land, presage excitements to come. Croisa stepped on the scene, beautiful as the fairest of Greek statues. She clasped her hands before her with the composure of one who commands her medium and embarked upon the intricacies of her program, drawing us far from the realities of place and time.

During the reception that came with the end of the music, guests were introduced to King Albert and Queen Elizabeth, monarchs admired for their learning, their sense of justice, their humanity. Watching them, as step by step I came near, observing their dignity, their grace, I reflected on these attributes and I lamented the fact that an inflexible situation drove these highly placed human beings away from the pleasures of every day and

pressed them into the narrow alleyways of cold duty.
Their Majesties could not, for example, be present on
that evening in Paris a few weeks later, when Madame
Croisa stood before our Pleyel piano and waited for her
accompanist to play the opening bars of Fauré's *Clair de
Lune*. I thought, as she sang, not only of royalty circum-
scribed but also of John Sargent, and I wondered
whether during the days when, in default of another
voice, he had hummed this melody to himself, he
dreamed of perfection such as this.

There was the encounter one day toward spring, as I
walked home along the Champs Élysées, with a funeral
cortege, slow, black, grave, a flow that seemed endless
and foreordained as the protracted unwinding of destiny.

"Who has died?" I asked a bystander.

"Ah, Madame, c'est Monsieur Fauré, compositeur."

I left the curb and stepped down to the highway, joining the mourners, following the body of the composer
on its ultimate journey. There were to be no more songs
written by that hand, written for the world, for Madame
Croisa, for John Sargent, for me, and I murmured a farewell. I remembered then another farewell, one forced
upon me, leaving the school where I had lived in England, that unhappy school such as Charlotte Brontë
described in *Jane Eyre*. There my little French protégée,
crippled, tragic, had come to count on me as a salvation
from bondage. But we were torn apart, never again to
meet, and the parting held the finality of death. Are we,
God's creatures, ever prepared to say the long good-by,
I asked myself, walking the pavement of the Champs
Élysées in step with the mourners.

15

LAST ENGAGEMENT

THE day came, many years after the death of my mother, long after the marriages of his three children, when my father lay stricken on his bed, when I hurried to the house of my childhood, the first of us three to arrive, summoned by the aging Irish retainer who had helped to bring us up, Minnie Gallagher, now my father's office nurse.

"I'm glad you've come so quick, Miss Gladys," Minnie said as she opened the front door. "The doctor's after leavin' the office to lie down. It's tired out he is. He had me to send the last patient away and I coaxed him into takin' off his clothes and gettin' to bed. You run on up now. It'll do him good to see you."

I hurried up the stairs, beneath the row of Japanese prints lining the wall, past the niche holding the bronze Mercury, and into my father's bedroom at the back of the house. He lay in his wide brass bedstead, the one he had slept in since I could remember.

"Well, Papa. How are you? Having a little rest?"

"That you, Gladys?"

I saw that he was wearing his white silk pajamas, those he kept for breakfast on Sunday mornings. It made his going to bed now, on a weekday, all the more out of the ordinary. His hair against the large square pillow was as white as the pajamas and his face was pale. He seemed very small and gentle.

"Haven't taken much time off in bed since you've known me, have I? Felt a trifle played out today, so I thought I'd lie still for a while."

"A good idea, Papa. You never stop working and running about. Don't you think it might be sensible to let a doctor see you?"

"No need for any nonsense like that. I can take care of myself a darn sight better than any stranger can."

"I only thought—" I stopped. Better not get him excited. "Have you been reading?" I picked up a book lying on the spread.

"Barrack-Room Ballads. Hadn't got around to reading yet but thought I might have a look at these later on. Kipling's a good man; knows how those poor chaps in India had to toe the mark: Danny Deever, Gunga Din. The early ones are the best."

"I'll read to you, if you like."

"I *would* like it. Hard for me to hold the book up and see clearly. Getting old, I guess, Gladys. Don't seem to be quite as strong as I was."

"You'll feel as strong as ever after a rest."

"It's the steady grind that plays you out. You get sick of pushing your way through the crowds in this city, and I've had just about enough of the damn fools who walk into my office every day. Now and then you come across a human being, but the common run is pretty low-grade stuff; keep you busy explaining things they've no business not to have found out for themselves."

He frowned fiercely but I knew from years of experience that the frown was meant for the damn fools and not for me. In a moment it disappeared and he smiled.

"I can remember lying in the meadows beside a brook when I was a boy, sticking my toes into the water and making a whistle out of a blade of grass. Not much of any time for that kind of thing these last years. You need a little relaxation as you grow older, but I don't seem to get much closer to a meadow than the grass I see in the vacant lots near the Yankee Stadium when I go to watch the ball games."

"We must see that you get more rest from now on. Think of all you've done, all the patients you've had, all the tonsils you've taken out."

"Yes, I've taken out a good many tonsils in my time, taken them out by the bushel, but it's all in the day's work. The longer I live, the more I dislike the fuss made over people who have nothing the matter with them. These nose and throat men coming along now send their patients to the hospital for a minor operation. Stuff and nonsense. Costs the patients a lot more; that's all they get out of it. Can't be done any better, most of it, than the way it's done right here in my office."

"Let me read to you now, Papa. You keep your eyes closed and forget about everything for a while. I'll read you 'Fuzzy-Wuzzy,' the one you read to me after you took out my adenoids that Sunday evening long ago when the blood spattered my best white organdy dress. Do you remember?" I turned the pages of the book,

reading the lines in a low voice, one eye on my father,
uncertain whether or not he followed the words:

So 'ere's *to* you, Fuzzy-Wuzzy, at your 'ome in the
    Soudan;
You're a pore benighted 'eathen but a first-class
    fightin' man. . . .

I finished the poem and my father opened his eyes
to smile once again. He lifted his hand and put it over
mine lying on the bed.

"I enjoyed that. Thank you, Gladys. I think I'll have
a short nap now. You're a good girl. Come back and see
me in the morning, if you will."

The clock on my bedside table pointed to midnight
when the light flashed suddenly on in the room which
had been my mother's room where I was spending the
night. Minnie's hand patted my shoulder.

"Wake up, Miss Gladys, dear. Your father's after
havin' a sinkin' spell. I've got a doctor in to see him and a
nurse from the Post Graduate Hospital." Minnie's voice
was tremulous.

Papa lay still in the big bed, shrunken, withdrawn,
perhaps asleep, and a doctor stood beside him holding his
pulse. Nearby, a nurse seemed already to have taken
possession and I stayed close to Minnie at the foot of the
bed. After a moment the doctor turned and beckoned
me. I followed him out of the room.

"I doubt if your father will pull through the night," he
said, standing at the head of the staircase. "His pulse is
erratic and his heart weak. I've given the nurse instruc-
tions. She knows where to reach me if I'm needed."

Curious how impersonal things became in the face of

the last finality. Strangers stepped in to take over and your very own parents ceased being a part of you, drawn off into a world that shut you out, a strange, far world that existed at no other time. I watched the doctor go down the stairs, then slowly I went back into the room. I drew up a chair at the side of the bed opposite the nurse and sat in silence, my eyes on my father. He looked so weak and helpless, so remote. He had rushed so all his life, gobbled his food, run up and down stairs, jumped onto moving streetcars. Now he was tired—too tired.

How sweet he had been that afternoon, I remembered with pleasure. How tender when he smiled and patted my hand, telling me I was a good girl. Now he was going to die, just as earlier my mother had been going to die. He did not belong to me any longer; he belonged to that capable starched nurse who sat holding his pulse and wetting his lips with a piece of damp gauze.

The nurse glanced across the bed. "You may as well go into another room and lie down," she said. "I'll call you if there's any change."

Obediently, I went into the library and stretched out on the sofa, arms over my head. It was a warm night and rain was falling. One of the windows was partly open and I lay listening to the sound of automobile tires sucking moisture as they turned and to the splash of flashing water jets against the mudguards. The room was in darkness save for a light on the big oak table, which was dimly reflected in the burnished curves of a copper bowl. I stared at the highlight as all the while my mind held fast to the image of the shrunken white figure at the other end of the hall.

Gradually, as I lay, an arm flung above my head, as in

childhood I had so often lain watching the firelight in my own room above, scenes from those early days floated into my mind, the days of Papa's vigor and swift attack. For he had never ceased in his striving to "get ahead," to "keep moving" toward a distant goal of his own contriving. He was a dynamo lubricated with the milk of human kindness. He had no use for the idlers, the stragglers; he had little use for any save those who "hustled" as he did. He attacked each day as during his boyhood he had attacked the after-school litter on the classroom floor, roof-high drifts of snow and, with his hand mower, the neighbor's grass. There, in Lee, Massachusetts, at ten, eleven, twelve, a small determined boy, he had accepted the debris scattered by man or the elements as his to deal with, as his to dispose of speedily, decisively, while the coins of his reward accumulated in inverse ratio to the scattering.

From the earliest moment Papa had wanted to save money in order to learn the profession of doctor. When on some fair day he became a doctor, he planned to look after those people who did not know how to look after themselves, those whom he pitied at the same time that he somewhat despised them. For the people he admired, to whom he was naturally drawn, were those who "pushed hard," who "attended to business," who avoided "nonsense." The others, those who "didn't know enough to come in when it rained," he would tend because they must be tended. The art of healing the sick was a part of teaching the ignorant to "have some sense." A pity, he felt, there were so many of these ignorant in the world, so many born with insufficient brains, insufficient guts, to cultivate a little sense. He never stopped trying to beat it into them.

In New York where Papa had gone to study medicine, where he set up finally a practice of his own in the diseases of the nose and throat, his habit of bestowing help, flinging it here and there on his swift passage, had endeared him to all who came near. It had begun with his first patients on Blackwell's Island when serving his internship at the prison hospital. There the men lined up for daily inspection.

"Say, Doc, me tooth's actin' up something dreadful. I ain't fit for road work." A rapid extraction with a pair of pliers, and the man was given a day off.

"Doc, will you please to look at me big toe, here? Not a step can I take for the pain of it."

And somehow the young doctor, sorting the chaff from the grain, managed to bring the semblance of hope to the hopeless. These were the men who remembered him later, out on parole or free again from restraint, who one by one rang the office doorbell and sat with the patients in the waiting room until it became their turn to enter the inner sanctum, there to deliver their presents in person to the youthful practitioner, to speak their gratitude and affection.

Other bonds of friendship my father continued to forge, many of these with professionals of the stage, whose performances before the difficult New York public largely depended upon the clarity, the suave functioning, of their voices. It had been his habit, when a cry for help from actor or singer sounded in his ears, to go forth in the evening after dinner carrying his small bulky doctor's satchel, to stand in the wings of the Lyceum or the Empire Theaters, or the Metropolitan Opera House, not only to be on hand in order to spray the ailing vocal cords but also to instill confidence and the proper attitude of attack into the performer's gesture.

"Ah, Doctor! You've pulled me up out of a worse spot than the Slough of Despond we read of," said a tall bass singer on the morning after he had successfully negotiated the role of King Mark in *Tristan and Isolde*. And he placed a hand upon my father's chunky shoulders as if to confer some high honor.

The ladies were grateful too: Julia Marlowe with her large dark eyes and well-modulated voice, Marie Tempest, arch and charming, the lovely Edna May in need of support during the long run of *The Belle of New York*. "Dear, dear Doctor," they said to him.

There were also the low-trodden individuals, those permanently down at the heel, the misfits, the deluded, the fanatical. Treating some of these with a frown on his brow, others with a genial slap on the back, Papa had taken them on as they came and came again, with little difference between his application to their needs and to those of the luckier ones, the opulent and the sophisticated. When a visit was ended he marked it down in his big office ledger. Only at the moment of mailing out the bills did the line appear as drawn between the rich and the poor.

"I've never charged a poor devil a cent more than he could pay," he once told me. "I'm not in favor of the large bills some doctors send out."

But all manner of presents, an attempt to square the circle, arrived at the office: a carriage robe of chinchilla, a violin in bad repair and later put in order for me as my first full-sized instrument; a scarf pin in the shape of a horseshoe with nails of diamonds; a paperweight of gleaming onyx, and many other offerings.

As for us, when we were children, we received rather more of the frown at moments of illness than the pat on the back. This meant that Papa was not sorry for us, that on the contrary, we had annoyed him. Illness was a falling from grace, a departure from the right, just as were the words misspelled in our school compositions. He counted on our hewing to the line, learning our lessons and keeping well. The frown inevitably appeared whenever we seemed to have capitulated to the disagreeable or the difficult.

"Get on your clothes and come up on deck," he ordered one day as I lay unhappily prone in my berth on board a transatlantic liner buffeted by equinoctial storms. "No use giving in to this thing. A few deep breaths of good fresh air will put you on your feet." But without the trust we had in him, we children and his patients, I doubt whether the cure could have been so entire.

My trust in my father affected my work and standing at school. Always he had made me feel that obstacles were there solely to be overcome. Sometimes, of an afternoon, driving about in a hansom cab to call on patients, he took me along that I might do my homework during the waits while he was inside the various houses. He would turn and nod, waving a hurried hand from the brownstone stoop before entering, a signal to me to set to work.

In summer, when we lived at East Hampton on Long Island, we left Papa with his patients and his office nurse, moving out with Mamma as soon as school ended. We moved with our Irish servants and King Arthur, the dignified high-stepping carriage horse who traveled in a box car on the train, attended by McCann, our cheerful, red-faced coachman. Our house was on a hill overlooking the sea three meadows away, and the smell of brine mingling with the smell of honeysuckle that climbed the piazza trellis, and the sound of breakers rolling everlastingly to the shore, made a perpetual background to paradise. From the balcony beyond our bedrooms Marjory and I watched the moonlight fall on daisy-filled meadows, we gathered mushrooms at dawn where cattle stood silently waiting for the light of day, and were saturated in sand and salt water under the noon sun. Concealed high among the branches of a cherry tree, safe from grownups while afternoon went toward evening, we ate the warm fruit as we read stories from Hawthorne and Bulwer-Lytton, or, taking turns, we drove our ex-stage pony Jack, blind in one eye but full of mettle still, along sandy lanes where scrub oak and pine fought each other for supremacy. After supper we lay out on couch or floor while the soft wind coming through open windows blew across the garden heliotrope, listening drowsily while Mamma read aloud. On chilly evenings, watching the great logs burning in the fireplace, the images made by licking flames wrought in our minds the pictures that illumined the words falling across the silence of the room.

Into these delights my father had plunged each Saturday and Sunday of the summer. He came by train late on a Friday afternoon and we children awaited him on the station platform. The New York City frown left his face at first glimpse of us, the doctor's satchel replaced by a carryall holding presents: a book, a bottle of cologne for my mother, a new garden trowel or a trap for killing moles and, for us, the box of Maillard's chocolates we knew in advance would be there. Presently, walking briskly along the platform, he seemed to have forgotten care as we moved toward the two-seated buckboard on the far side of the station where McCann in whipcord jacket and chamois breeches held the reins over King Arthur.

But peace did not penetrate any great distance into the week's end. Soon after the second cup of Saturday morning coffee, my father was outdoors in the garden at work on the weeds which had had their way during the week just past.

"Come out here and give me a hand," he would call to one of us. "We'll be through before you can say 'Jack Robinson' if we put our minds on this job."

Mamma, on these mornings, was up in her bedroom, beyond the open casement, having her breakfast from a tray and reading Herbert Spencer. Among us children, still eating our oatmeal in the dining room, Durant was too small to be good at weeding and Marjory was intent on her after-breakfast visit to the stable with lumps of sugar for the horses. So it was I, usually, who responded to my father's first morning ardor, working beside him on my knees, dirt beneath my nails and around the edges of my mouth, my hair damp with perspiration, my spirit on the wane long before I was allowed to pause.

Cutting the grass was another of my father's enthusiasms. He pushed the mower before him as though conveying a miscreant to final punishment. Each stubborn blade became an enemy, and the frown seldom left his brow while he walked to and fro bareheaded beneath the hot sun, round and round the wide geranium bed in the center of the driveway, up and down the hill that led to the entrance gate. The frown was caused in part by his annoyance with the boy who came two days a week supposedly to keep the grass down, an inept boy of whom Papa spoke as "half-baked."

Once, when the morning work had ended, the whirr of mower blades suddenly gone dead, my father had returned from the tool shed, pale under the clinging damp of the heat, a big white handkerchief falling limp from his hand.

"Guess I overdid things a bit just now," he said, entering the house. "I'll go and stretch out for a while."

When Mamma suggested sending for the doctor, my father's black eyes gleamed with anger. "Stuff and nonsense!" he exclaimed. "That chap won't tell you a thing I couldn't tell you myself."

The doctor arrived presently and said that Papa had had a sunstroke, that cool compresses should be kept on his brow and that he should take things more easily.

"I don't believe in taking things easily," my father said when the doctor had gone. "What a young greenhorn! I'll be all right after I have a short nap."

It was with a good deal of relief to us all, during those summers, in spite of our love for our father, when after the departure of the Sunday evening train we could once more become aware of the quiet, dormant things, the tang of salt on the easterly breeze, the sound of the cricket on our tranquil evening hearth. A relief to Papa also, it must have been, on his way back to the city streets, to the office, to the disorder and the stresses of his own

kingdom wherein his patients were ever his willing
vassals doing trustful homage to their sovereign.

In sudden terror I roused myself from my dreams, and
moving to the lamp to look at my watch found that I
had slept for two hours. Without waiting to put on my
shoes I ran along the hall and into Papa's room. The
nurse was in the same position at the side of the bed. It
might have been two minutes rather than two hours
later except for the difference in the way my father was
breathing. He drew in cruel, jagged, suffering breaths
and let them go again with a sigh that pressed down
down, to the very bottom of his being. A kind of dragon's breathing it was, a dragon with a spear in its side.
I wondered how the nurse could sit there without concern as though this thing fallen upon my father was a
natural thing. Why didn't she take part in the mortal
combat, help the man beside her?

Then I remembered, and, remembering, went to sit in
an armchair away from the bed. This was the way people
breathed just before they died. It was natural because it
was the way most human beings had to breathe before
they stopped entirely. My mother had breathed that way
until, finally, she had become the strange stiff creature I
had found so difficult to recognize, lying more still than
she had ever lain in a box too narrow for her eager
gesture, her hands crossed, as she would never have had
them, like the hands of a saint, on her breast. That had
not been my mother, and now, soon, this struggling man
would not be my father. This last engagement he was
keeping with an unknown person at so great a cost
would come to an end and he would be off on his solitary, most private business.

I wanted with all my might to say good-by to him once more before it was too late, to kneel beside him, tell him I had always loved him even though, since my marriage, I seemed so far away, tell him that I thanked him, that I would remember him always. I started up from my chair —no, it was already too late. I dropped back and put my two hands over my face with fingers pressed tight against my eyes.

Then, deliberately, I summoned the picture of a small sturdy man carrying a bulging black satchel in his hand. As he disappeared into the doorway of a brownstone house, he looked back to wave at a little girl seated in a hansom cab below, her hat ringed with daisies on the back of her head and a schoolbag in her lap.

At the edge of the grave, I turned my head to watch Durant. He stared with absent eyes and solemn mouth, staring as though trying to remember what he had lost. This was the way he had stared at the tapestry hanging in the hall of our house when I had found him, a small boy, years ago, seated on the carved oak bench as I came in from an afternoon in Gramercy Park. He had lost the frontispiece to his sailor suit and been forbidden to move until he recollected where he had left it. This was the way he watched the world as it turned him about. I put an arm through his.

Beyond the raw cavity dug from the green of the cemetery grass there was a lilac bush, its buds swollen and alive. How curious, I thought, that it would presently bloom with exuberance in this spot set apart to mark the dead. All the rest was strange, uncouth, a game with rules transposed from some nightmare, these rites forced upon us now, upon my sister, my brother and me. Upon my father also. For he could never have lain there without protest while men and women with stiffly cast faces, funeral faces, looked stonily on.

Marjory stood a little beyond us, nearer to the others, to those strangers who had come through the mysterious right of relationship, a herd of black appearing now in intimacy as they had not done while Papa lived. Marjory was kind, or perhaps it was that she did not feel herself apart. She stood now beside these people, magnificently upright, her great eyes, with their look of tragedy, darker than her dark dress. She seemed a regal personage, and I thought of the time when we were young, when our friend Tommy Safford had called her the "Moldavian Princess."

The last of the clergyman's words went off into the damp spring wind, the last blue iris on the coffin bowed its head beneath the gravediggers' shovels, the line of mourners lost its precision, men in officious black sprang to open the doors of shining black limousines, engines unobtrusively murmuring, and into one of these we climbed, my father's three children, while Minnie Gallagher entered to sit on one of the small seats, as befitted her rank of service. Minnie's service to the Rice family had extended for so many years that we felt her to be an integral part of us, but, although Durant had motioned her to the rear seat beside Marjory and me, she had refused to comply. Her face was swollen with crying and her mouth wavered at the corners. Her brown rosary was in her hands, the rosary I had known during years too long to count. Lucky Minnie! She would always and forever have this friend to comfort her.

The funeral car swung into Riverside Drive. We sat without speaking, without moving, until Durant leaned forward to let down one of the windows. A breeze tore free a lock of my hair, and I thought of the drives we had taken here along this street as children returning from picnics, with Mamma clinging in the wind to her hat and Papa stiffly upright, whip in hand, in the yellow buckboard behind King Arthur clumping on and on, while we dozed against our parents' shoulders, waking with a jump when the boat whistles on the river blew sudden and shrill.

At the house, Minnie left us to change into her uniform, as though to continue with duties from which fate had forever severed her, and we went into the drawing room. There Marjory and I sank deep into the crimson velvet cushions of the gilt sofa, the one Mamma had brought back from France, the one on which she sat when her Thursday afternoon friends came to tea, pouring cherry bounce for the ladies from a delicate Venetian glass decanter after they put their teacups down. Durant faced us, back to the door.

The room was all my mother; everything in it came finally back to her, to her warmly encompassing taste, to the thing she had been, the words she had spoken. I remembered that once, sitting here with my husband after our honeymoon, this room had seemed dim, almost dilapidated, alongside the brilliant, polished places in which I was being taken to live. But now this house, this drawing room in particular, shone forth again in its full worth as the symbol of all I had thought valuable throughout the years: the rugs trodden by the feet of friends, faded in the sunshine that fell as it liked, as a dog

falls to rest; the wandering pink and blue veins of the
marble mantel, like the veins of a lovely lady; the height
of the tall windows and the height of the tall mirror
reaching from floor to ceiling and confronting the table
that held a dancing Tanagra figure flanked by a pair of
Sheffield plate candlesticks, their silver blurred by the
copper beneath. There was the dim velvet of chair cover
ings worn with the weight of human beings who had sat
slumped beneath the burden that life imposed, and
along a wide space of wall, the shaded leaves and flower
of a woven verdure tapestry brought an added sense of
shelter to all else.

The grand piano stood, as usual, close to the entrance
its case stained and dented, its bulging legs a bulwark
of support for generations of fingers running along its
yellowed keys. Often in the past, it had been a support
to me when I practiced my violin pieces with Tommy
Safford, who accompanied and coached me at the same
moment, in order that I might do my best at our Sunday
evening parties when Mamma counted on me to play
for her friends: Massenet's "Meditation" from *Thaïs*
Hubay's "Zephyr," Bach's "Air on the G String." Papa
came running down the small curved staircase from his
office at the back of the house, on those evenings when
his work was done, and he clapped louder than all the
rest, crying, "Bravo! Bravo!" Then in a loud voice he
would call out, asking me to play some piece of a not too
distinguished kind or one I had grown tired of playing
This embarrassed me a good deal, but in my deepest
heart I was glad my father approved of my playing
even though I knew I did not deserve quite so much
enthusiasm. Later, when I had reached sixteen or so,

Tommy and I discarded these simple pieces, adaptations for the violin as many of them were, and we came to rely on the sonatas composed by the great: Schubert, Mozart, Beethoven, Brahms. Then, I noticed, Papa came in less often, clapped with less zest. He had lost his familiar friends.

My father was proud of Durant's playing too, the playing we gathered about the piano to hear when he was a young man home from Harvard, home later from the Mexican border and again from serving in the American Ambulance Corps early in the First World War. Durant's whole life had been interspersed with martial adventure, with the discipline and courage of the warrior. Yet, the music he made was deeply moving: the sound of his poignant voice singing to an accompaniment of his own contriving upon the keys, without the aid of printed notes. He sang the songs of the French people, songs that were ageless, beginning with the child's *Chansons de France,* from the book illustrated by Boutet de Monvel containing *Malbrough s'en va en guerre, Au clair de la lune, Savez-vous planter les choux?* continuing with the love songs of the Paris pavements. Once, I remembered, when Durant spent an evening with my husband and me making music in our house, I went suddenly into the pantry, and there, close to the door, in tears, I found our young French cook who had not been long in America.

"Ah, Madame," she sobbed when I questioned her, *"cette belle musique me fait penser à mon frère qui fut tué à la guerre."* This was the kind of power Durant possessed. He was able in his music to remind us of all the sadness, the tenderness, lying dormant in our hearts.

A hand organ interrupted my thought, flinging its

wavering dissonance against the luster pendants of the drawing room chandelier.

"Do you suppose it's the man with the fedora hat and the curled mustache and the sad wife?" I asked Durant. "The ones we gave our nickels to when we were small?"

"It must be their son," he answered solemnly, in the way that he had.

"I used to try and keep time to the rhythms of the hurdy-gurdy on my roller skates, I remember."

"And do you remember the election night bonfires of those days? How exciting they were!" Marjory said.

"A lot of strenuous work beforehand, for our crowd, salvaging the barrels from empty lots and excavations, storing them in back yards to keep them away from the gang."

"The gang, the Fourteenth Street Gang. They were a tough lot."

"Gave me a bloody nose more than once," said Durant.

"Papa used to put you in the Morris chair in his office with the bar let down so that your head fell far back, to stop the bleeding."

"I brought you lumps of ice from Nellie's kitchen icebox wrapped in a napkin," Marjory recollected, "and the water made little channels in the dirt around your mouth."

Durant smiled in the reflective way that people have when they dwell on a happy past.

"We had twenty-five or thirty barrels each year," he said.

"The largest fire within ten city blocks, a huge pyramid. Marjory and I used to watch you from the bow window in the library. Flames shot halfway up the brownstone fronts and we were always afraid the fire engines might be called out. I can remember how hard it was to get to sleep afterwards."

"Kids don't seem to have that sort of freedom today," Durant said, "our kind of kids, at any rate. They join the Boy Scouts or they're sent off to school away from the city, and the aggressive instinct is frowned upon. Probably a good idea. I don't know. But I do know I enjoyed the battles in those days, win or lose, and the return to base and safety which was this house of ours."

He stopped. The past had laid its hand upon him to overwhelm and silence him, to silence us all, as, earlier in the day, we had been brought into the great silence that confronts death.

We sat together, two sisters and a brother, while the wheezy, jerky notes of the old hurdy-gurdy came from afar to blend with the memories of childhood, to summon pain and pleasure in that tender mingling which men name nostalgia.

16

---◆◆---

A SPRING DAY

A FORSYTHIA bush on the lawn close by the steps of the Presbyterian Church on lower Fifth Avenue was spread with yellow, and across the way a row of hyacinths, pink and white blossoms of meticulous stiffness, lined the iron fence that bounded a wide brick house. I had seen them earlier, had watched them in the progress of their spring effort, but today, under the steady sun and the quiet windless warmth, they were without flaw, their effort had ceased.

I took a few running steps, my head turned toward the direction from which I had come. A bus from Washington Square was approaching the stop at the corner above. I must hurry if I was to board it. I looked again. No room on top. The benches open to sun and air were already filled to the very last seat with contented people. Never mind. I would walk. Plenty of minutes ahead. The opera was not to begin for more than an hour and I felt well enough, with enough energy, to walk to Grant's Tomb.

I had felt well and almost truly happy from the moment of opening my eyes that morning to look beyond the balcony overhanging the yard of my small flat in West Eleventh Street, where a young ginkgo tree held its leaves like a fan to be unfurled with the very next wave of heat, to hear the man in the street below who walked beside his slow-wheeled wagon crying, "Plants for sale!" and to smell—actually to smell from where I lay in my bed beneath the window—spring turning then and there into summer. A fine thing to feel happiness again even though it might be a happiness less assured, less resolute, than that of former days when I had thought to keep grief forever at arm's length, days before the fall. The words of the old nursery rhyme flashed through my mind:

> Humpty Dumpty sat on a wall.
> Humpty Dumpty had a great fall.
> All the King's horses and all the King's men
> Couldn't put Humpty together again.

Before falling from high atop of my wall, I had looked down on a kingdom wherein lay riches and adulation and willing service and the myth of endless continuity. Round about me were my children, my love for them, theirs for me, warm, encompassing. Now I was alone, had been alone throughout the long, long winter months, months sprung from an autumn which I had not recognized in its bright essence because of my removal from accustomed things: the maples hanging scarlet above the Ipswich River in a Massachusetts valley, the great quiet oak on the hillside beyond our house steadfast in its splendor, the golden flutter of aspen and poplar when the breeze tossed leaves groundward. I was removed also from my children, from their trust and their immense need of me, as the season prepared for chill winds, prepared for the annual drowning of a world in ice and snow. Who had been there to see to the purchase of warm underclothing, to make sure their suits and galoshes were whole and intact? Who, during the months since I had left Boston, had listened to their recitations of poetry learned for school, bent over their desks at evening to help with the solving of arithmetic problems? My children—they were always and forever in my mind, the eldest in boarding school, the three younger ones tended by strangers in a strange land.

Boston—a place that had long enfolded me, blessed me, a place become a part of me, a place I had loved. How I missed the sunsets spread wide and free over the Charles River basin, the tubs of spring flowers set out on Beacon Hill house steps, the leisurely friendliness of passersby in the street. Boston—now no more than a name on the map; Kamchatka, Keokuk, were other names on the map and equally remote. "Boston and Return," the ticket read, purchased at the window of the New Haven railroad in the Grand Central Station. Boston and Return signified a round trip, a going and a coming back. That was the ticket I had used. How strange! How difficult, how impossible to understand.

But now at last, winter had gone and spring was in the air. Would difficulties lessen, understanding deepen, with the presence of soft winds blowing, with the promise of summer on ahead when I should be reunited with the children at Martha's Vineyard by the sea? We had always been happy at the seashore, the children and I.

There was the summer spent at Houlgâte in France. This was the summer when Jean was still a baby while the older ones received with wide and solemn interest their first impression of lands far from home. My husband, during that summer, raced his three-meter boat against the Europeans in the waters off Cowes on the Isle of Wight. He came and went between France and England, taking me with him once or twice to watch the races. Between these visits I was with the children much of the time on the long white sands of the beach, and it was here, playing with the small French children, that mine learned to speak the language. I remembered the afternoon when Jock had been terror-stricken by an inebriate but poetic Frenchman who walked beside the waves crying, *"La mer est ma mère!"* As the little boy ran into my arms, I was able to calm him, saying, "That man has no mother, so he begs the sea to be his mother. You have a mother close beside you, so you don't have to cry."

Summer would come again, next summer. Then the children would have a mother once more and their mother would have them. Not too many months to wait. Meanwhile I must endure loneliness as best I could, the melancholy sense of separation. Also the unnatural strain of organized separation from a husband, a cord hanging frayed and limp yet persisting with stubborn tenacity to outworn use. Dreadful to sever the past, to destroy stores of good along with the less good. Destruction. How malevolent a business! I had always been moved to sadness at the leveling of a patient old house by workmen with crowbars and drills, men setting lustily to work while seeming to take a savage pleasure in the crashing and the tumbling. Every now and then the process brought a display of privacies laid bare, the exposure of some room not intended for public inspection, a library papered in dun-colored obscurity, its empty shelves gaping at the sudden intolerable light. This was the mode usual to annihilation whether of inanimate or animate objects. I was among the latter, and the sudden illumination of privacies, dun-colored or otherwise, had brought bewilderment edged with sorrow.

Ahead at the next corner, as I walked with rapid stride making my way uptown, I saw a basement flower shop. A bowl in the window was filled with yellow primroses. I veered toward it, ran the two steps down and went inside. I chose a small bunch from among the others and fastened it to my jacket.

"No odor, but the color is irresistible," I murmured half aloud. "A lovely day," I said to the florist as he came near.

"Yes, indeed. Makes you want to be in the country."

I smiled in acquiescence. "You're lucky," I said. "All these flowers around you. But I have a back yard."

The florist smiled now. "Come again, Miss."

I liked to be called "Miss." It made me feel as though, along with the sidewalk children, I too might skip rope or roll a hoop.

Outside, I determined on the course I was to take to the Metropolitan Opera House. The opera to be sung on this Saturday afternoon was Debussy's *Pelléas and Mélisande*. I knew it well from the days when I had heard it sung at the Opéra Comique in Paris: an old friend, now to bring acquaintance renewed. There were fifty clear minutes ahead, I saw. I could walk the distance easily in that time. I would go west on Thirty-fourth Street and continue on up Broadway, through pushing crowds, becoming for a while a part of the unfamiliar world that pivots about Times Square.

Reaching Thirty-fourth Street, before turning west, I had a sudden desire to see the shrubs in flower about Mr. Morgan's house on Madison Avenue and Thirty-ninth Street. I had always enjoyed walking past that house in springtime when I was young, when Mr. Morgan was still alive. Years ago, I had been invited there to a dance, one of the high marks of my youth, high mark in the sense of pure joy in living, in dancing to the decisive rhythm of a fine band, of flirting with a variety of partners and later, as the evening wore beyond midnight, in acceding to the delightful attentions of a handsome young man. During a waltz, on that evening, as I was swung by my partner in wide slow movement about the floor, a taffeta bag, a cotillion favor hanging by a ribbon to my arm, was flung off into space, the ribbon come unsewn.

"Never mind," my partner said as I paused. "Wait till the music stops. It's too good to miss."

"But my gold pencil favor is inside that bag," I answered, "the pencil with the jeweled screw. I'd rather not lose it."

"We'll find it all right. Don't worry." And his arm held me closer as we entered the rhythm of the waltz again.

When the music halted we approached a footman standing at attention nearby.

"Did you see a silk bag that fell from this young lady's

arm?" my partner asked.

"It had a gold pencil inside," I added, helping to identify it.

The man appeared to be in doubt. "I'll look around," he said finally. Presently he returned, the bag in his hand.

"That's it," I said. "The ribbon is unsewn, you see."

"There's no gold pencil inside it, not that I can find anyways, Miss."

"Oh, but I'm sure—" I stopped short, suddenly confronted with the sense of irreparable loss, with the outrage and despair that the act of theft brings to the victim.

Today, pausing to look at the azaleas and the lilacs that held their buds open on the far side of the railing around the Morgan grounds, I remembered that faraway episode and I remembered a conversation that ensued a few days after the party between my mother and Mrs. Edward Hewitt, her intimate friend. We were drinking tea, the three of us, before the library fire in our house on Irving Place, and Mamma had just finished telling Mrs. Hewitt the story of the party at Mr. Morgan's and of its disappointing outcome for me.

"You must make a point of reading about conspicuous waste in Veblen's book, *The Theory of the Leisure Class,* Gladys. That should bring things into better focus for you," said Mrs. Hewitt, whose viewpoint was that of a bluestocking and not to be lightly brushed aside.

"Yes," Mamma agreed, "all that luxury and lavish entertainment floating about: an inducement, even though of the wrong kind, for those on the outside to try for a share."

Sagacity of this sort, if not entirely comforting to a girl of eighteen, was cause for reflection, and the image of the pencil with jeweled screw faded, somewhat, in luster.

What, I wondered, thinking back on that far time, would my mother have said to me today? As to riches and lavish display, I agreed with her and with Mrs. Hewitt. Varying degrees existed, of course, in the possession of wealth and the manner of its usage. There in Boston, ostentation played no part in our way of life, yet I had had domain over a large household while almost any wish of mine for possessions or for entertainment came true as if by means of a fairy's fertile wand. But what a load to carry! Heavy, awkward, endlessly growing in the manner of spores self-induced: the complex machinery of the household to keep running, the various and often dissenting personalities to manage among the staff, the continual need for choice in a complex world where, in spite of luxury and apparent ease, leisure and peace seemed a dream forever out of reach.

How pleasant, by contrast, how fine and free, to greet the new morning in one's own small and most private kitchen where a pot of everlasting, a countrywoman's flower, stands on the breadbox in a south window, where the amber of floor paint echoes the gold of the sunshine from the yard beyond. How light, compared with former burdens, the weight of the paper bag of groceries, sufficient for the day, borne in one's arms home from the corner store.

Would Mamma have encouraged or condemned me in this most recent existence? What would have been her understanding, what her pleasure or possible despair, in my present state of suspension? Would she view it as a fall from grace? Wonderful to have her beside me at this moment, to speak, to guide. I recollected the talks we had had in the past on the subject of marriage, when I told her of my fear of being unable to love any one human being throughout all the years of life. Her reply to these doubts had been a challenge: "Love depends on you and your own soul." Had my soul, in permitting me to go away—to concede that unhappiness was stronger than love—brought abandonment of the fair attributes she envisioned, the attributes that God must surely have sought in me? Yet how unwilling I had been on that last evening before the wedding. How I had longed to close the door against the future. How sad, how terror-stricken, during the final chill night of maidenhood when, shivering from cold, I had said good-by to the familiar things, to the rowboat on the pond beneath the willow, to the inkwell on my desk, its gilt glimmering under the moonlight that slanted across the window ledge.

During the years of marriage I had attempted to stifle fear once and for all, to push away the undercurrents of sadness. But these signs of frailty, pointing to a child-hood not outgrown, had clung fast in spite of all the insight gained through bearing and guiding children of my own, in spite of the security brought by my sur-roundings. Thus I remained uncertain of my direction although I felt a continual gratitude for the wide leeway and the very great patience my husband bestowed on me as I trod my path of single choosing. How irksome for a man, I thought now, a heavy load of guilt weighing upon my heart, how wearisome to have had to tolerate the spectacle, endlessly renewed, of a wife ever eager to explore, eager for fresh fields, asking questions of one person and yet another in the search for fullness, for wisdom, in the need to learn, to sense, to feel. Especially when this particular man, descendant of his shipping forebears with their galleons under sail across the oceans of the world, had less of a taste for human exchange than for the silence of night beneath the stars, days of windless drifting, dreams of eternity in the great solitude that is the sea.

Times Square slowed my pace, slowed my thought, as I joined the determined flow of a Saturday afternoon. Couples strolled in intimacy; women walked alone, eyes on the alert for conquest; women in threes or fours, rigidly waved hair like structures wrought in iron, cheeks indelibly rouged, emerged in bulk from Schrafft's on their way to a matinee; girls gazed into the broad curved windows of shoe stores; young men with wide-shouldered, belted jackets stood against lampposts, nonchalantly smoking; mothers and sons from out of town clung to each other frowning, afraid of missing what they had come for. I stared and wondered, and the desolation, the haunting loneliness which had briefly left me in the delight of a spring morning, returned now to engulf me.

Broadway pressed into the front lobby of the Opera House, a milling, chattering mass, and with difficulty I forced a path to the gate. Inside, a beneficent hush followed me as I moved along muffled aisles to my place in the orchestra. Sitting there in padded spaciousness beneath the semicircle of buttressed red-and-gold boxes above my head, their twinkling lights a fairylike contrast to the brilliance of sunshine left behind, I felt as though touched by the quality of a chimera. I gave myself en-

tirely to the dream, pressing deeper into my seat, waiting,
separate, detached, until at last the great house murmured with the presence of many other human beings
such as I.

The lights went out and with a sudden vibration of
strings, striking an almost mortal blow, the orchestra
began Debussy's overture. I closed my eyes while the
tender portions of my being opened to the music, just
as, in ways foreordained, a lily opens to noon sunshine.
I listened to the thing the instruments proclaimed, beauty
bound round with sorrow, which was what I had chiefly
known, had always known, and the whole of reality now
was but the throbbing of my pulse in unison with it.

I watched the scenes as they unfolded, remembering
them as I had seen them in other years. I watched the
fair Mélisande seated in innocence beside her husband's
mother in a window overlooking the sea, as she heard
the reading of a letter which announced the coming of
Pelléas: a timid, affrighted Mélisande caught like some
fluttering bird off the branch. I watched and agonized
for Mélisande when her husband in fearful jealousy
dragged her along the floor, dragged her by her braided
hair, flung her to right, flung her to left, again and yet
again.

"I am not happy!" she cried, and I cried with her, remembering the tragedy of the whole world as the storm-
tossed Mélisande uttered her piteous lament.

I watched and listened to the rapture of Pelléas as he
stood below his love in a window high above and
stroked her golden hair, its mass flowing down about
him: peace before the violence of tempests. In horror I
saw the attempted destruction of Pelléas by his brother

at the border of a dark lagoon far below the ground, and I drew a breath of happiness when, out in the sunshine once more, he stretched forth his arms to welcome the light, singing, *"Oh, la clarté. . . ."* while the stridency of accompanying sound smote the air, tearing it asunder, tearing my heart asunder.

Never, before today, had the meeting of lovers at the fountain been as passionate, as grave, as hopeless. They stood, each binding the other in unheeding finality, while the moon bathed them in its stark white light. They waited, and I waited with them, for the sword thrust which was to wrest the kisses of Pelléas from Mélisande, drive them away for all time as she ran, ran, ran from things too great to bear. And the harmonies that gathered about them during their last supreme moment fused a perfection of loveliness evanescent as the mirage of magnified flowers that now and then illumined my dreams.

Outside, enveloped in the mellow glow of afternoon, I found my legs were weak and I walked unevenly, bumping people a little as I had done, I remembered, after listening to Ysaye play the violin years ago when I was a child. I hailed a cab and sank into a corner, letting the window beside me drop all the way. I was tired because of the moments of high emotion that had enveloped me. I was glad to be tired. I did not want to lose the power of feeling acutely. During some of the years now left behind I had been deprived of that power, and the apathy come to take its place had been difficult to bear. Life was made of suffering and joy. They took turns. Suffering I had known throughout the months just passed, known in the full force of its power to attack. I had forever lost a part of myself. I should not be put together again as before, in the same way, with the same ingredients.

But if, as some said, history unravels backward, if the end looks toward the beginning, it was written in the Book of Fate that I should once again be able to mingle the earnest striving of childhood, the innocence, the happy dreams, with the current of my life.

"Let me not forget these things, dear God. Let me remember joy. And let me remember goodness."

I spoke the words aloud as the driver slowed his taxi beside the Presbyterian Church. There, on the lawn, its gold intense under the falling sun, the forsythia bush shone out in glory.

GLADYS BROOKS

"I was born during the 'gay nineties' in a house on Irving Place in New York," writes Gladys Brooks. The office of her father, a throat specialist, was at the rear of the house, and his patients, the actors and singers of the day, arrived in horse-drawn cabs and entered around the corner on Nineteenth Street. As a small girl, Mrs. Brooks roller-skated on Irving Place, passing the gabled house where Washington Irving once lived, the factory where the famous Huyler chocolates were made, the Minsky Burlesque Theatre and the Academy of Music, with its vivid posters that displayed terrifying melodramas. Educated at the Brearley School in New York and by governesses in France, Mrs. Brooks later interrupted her studies in landscape gardening at the Arnold Arboretum in Brookline, Massachusetts, to marry. During the next fifteen years she lived in Boston and bore four children. When she and her husband were separated, she returned to New York City. "The most recent fifteen years of my life," states Mrs. Brooks, "have been happily influenced by my marriage to Van Wyck Brooks, with whom I live in an architecturally awkward but hospitable house . . . in a small Connecticut village." This house, with its hedge-enclosed garden at the rear, is to Mrs. Brooks "a refuge from the passing scene and . . . point of safe return."